MILLIONAIRE

SUCCESS SECRETS

MILLIONAIRE
SUCCESS SECRETS

Pressman House

ADAM STOTT

Pressman House

ISBN 978-1-913839-57-4

(Also available as an eBook ISBN 978-1-915657-34-3)

MMXXIII

A CIP catalogue record for this book
is available from the British Library

Published by
Pressman House Publishing Ltd, Boston, Lincs,
PE20 3BT   England
Tel: +44 (0) 1296695588
www.pressman-house.co.uk

Foreword

By Charlie Mullins OBE

Like a lot of people in business, I have a few tales to tell. Some good, a few bad. Experiences that I've had, which transformed themselves into little nuggets of advice that have proven to be useful to others.

There is a misguided belief that the journey of an entrepreneur is a lonely one. For me, it's a complete misconception.

Common sense tells you anyone who tries to do anything without the advice and guidance of those who have been there and done it are doomed to failure.

It's so important to surround yourself with people with more experience and skills than you.

I apply the same principle to apprentices – I would always pair them with my longest-serving engineers at Pimlico Plumbers so they could gain the knowledge and 'tricks of the trade' they would never gain in a classroom.

An entrepreneur can't be expected to know or do everything, having the right team is vital, but it also helps you gain more of an understanding of how a business should be run.

What the entrepreneur brings is that spark of ingenuity, the drive to succeed and the tenacity to overcome any setback.

And learning from other entrepreneurs is a key part of achieving business success, whether it's through formal mentoring, or just simply listening to those who have walked the path before you.

Undoubtedly Adam is one of those people. When we first met, he was keen to tell me how my book had influenced him and how important learning and mentorship from people who had been there, done that and got the t-shirt was to a young entrepreneur.

Despite Adam being an Essex boy rather than a South Londoner like me I see a lot of me in him. He pulled himself up by his bootstraps, despite his early years being disrupted by family problems, and through hard work, determination and soaking up as much information from as many sources as possible, he has made something of himself.

And, as life has a habit of repeating itself, he is also doing what all good entrepreneurs should do, helping others on their business journeys.

This book tells Adam's story, without glossing over the mistakes he has made. He shares many of the life and business lessons he has learned which makes it essential reading for anyone with aspirations to start, or grow a business.

He speaks a lot of common sense, so take it in, because in my experience common sense ain't that common.

Introduction:

By The author.

Books have made a major impact on my life. I have read thousands. This book is the one I wish I'd found at the beginning of my journey. I have written it for readers who want more from their lives, but perhaps haven't quite figured out how to connect the dots. People who want to make changes.

Perhaps you've experienced highs and lows in your journey. Maybe you're at the very beginning, or perhaps you've already celebrated some successes.
If any of these scenarios resonate with you, this book has the potential to transform your path and guide you toward implementing meaningful change, regardless of what drives you.

In the following pages I will share with you the lessons I learned on my way from a broke teenager with no prospects who had been written off and forgotten, to a millionaire who loves life and now helps thousands of others to make the same transformative journey.

I want you to use this book to accomplish your goals, dreams and ambitions faster and without the ups and downs so you can start living your dream life.

I want to make it clear; I don't have any special talent. I don't have the genes of success. I've been down and I've failed. At times in my life, I had nothing. I worked my way up from the bottom, my first job was frying chicken in a takeaway shop. I tell you this not to impress or to boost my ego; I tell you this because I believe that if I can do it, you can do it too, regardless of where you are starting from.

Although I possess no superpowers, I've honed the skill of simplifying complex concepts into easy, user-friendly systems, thanks to experience and invaluable mentorship. These systems transform ordinary individuals into the extraordinary, and this book is a compilation of them.

In the following pages you will discover systems that show you how to:

- Dramatically increase your income
- Get clarity and avoid confusion
- Avoid becoming overwhelmed
- Stop procrastinating
- Manage fear and risk
- Act faster
- Boost your profile and reputation
- Build relationships with powerful people
- Market yourself, your products and services
- Get known and stand out
- Sell products and services, even if you hate sales and are afraid of rejection
- Create a strategy to start businesses and increase your income
- Brand and position yourself so you stand out in crowded markets

My aim is to give you a playbook to become successful. This includes all the tools and secrets you'll need to go from where you are now to becoming a millionaire.

Start your journey with dedication and remember this: Too many books are bought and never finished.
Commit to reading and revisiting this book several times. The key to the changes you want in your life is contained in these pages, go through it with a highlighter and pick out the lessons that apply to you the most. I've included bullet points to highlight the key lessons at the end of each biographical chapter to help you.

My commitment to producing this book is to go all-in to serve you as much as I possibly can. My ambition is to create many new millionaires and successful people. I want you to be one of them.

And the commitment doesn't stop there. When you've read the book head over to my website, *www.adamstott.com* where the journey continues and where you can access 350+ podcast episodes on building a business, plus virtual training events on social media marketing and business growth. You can also find out how to work with me personally in my programmes.

I hope this is one of those books that makes a major difference in your life and sets you on a new path to achieving everything you want.

You are about to go on a wild ride.

Enjoy,
Adam

Contents

MILLIONAIRE

SUCCESS SECRETS

1

The Journey Begins. Starting Out on Success

Every successful person starts from somewhere, usually at the bottom of the pile from where they work their way up through hard graft, guile, cunning, and a bit of luck. It's an old cliché, but every journey really does begin with a single step.

And for the purposes of this book – which tells the story of my journey to success and gives valuable lessons that will help you on your journey – my first step was both a physical step, and a symbolic one because when I think about my lowest point and the place from where I started, I think about a step in a house in Essex.

The house was a mess. It was being renovated and had practically been torn down by my dad, who was a builder. There was no heating, no front door, no windows. It was cold, damp, and filthy. It was covered in dust and bits of rubble. The step I am talking about was the bottom stair in the hallway.

I was sixteen years old, sitting on it, feeling absolutely miserable and wishing I could be anywhere else.

It was my first job. I was fresh out of school and the thrill of having left the educational environment that I was never suited to had worn off as soon as I realised that the reality of working life for someone like me – a tearaway teen hooligan without a single qualification – was either on a cold building site or in a call centre somewhere.

My dad realised that as I was unqualified and unmotivated, my career options were limited so he gave me some work as a labourer. I hated every single second of it. I was the world's most reluctant employee. Previously, I'd been a typical teenager, sleeping all day, going out all night, doing nothing apart from misbehaving with my mates. I had no idea what I wanted to do with my life and the only thing I really knew was that I didn't want to work with my dad as a labourer. Consequently, I did everything I could to avoid doing any work. This is why I was sitting on the stairs, counting the specks of rubble on the tattered, threadbare carpet. Skiving.

Occasionally one of the other workers would step over me and tut or comment on my lack of enthusiasm and inaction. Or Dad would want some help and call me; in which case I'd drag myself up with zero eagerness and trudge off to see what he wanted. I was as lackadaisical as it was possible to be. I didn't want to carry anything I didn't want to lift anything, I didn't want to clear anything up and I didn't want to get my hands dirty or break a sweat. I wanted to be anywhere other than there. I was bored beyond belief!

If this is what work is like, I thought to myself, *I don't want to do it.*

My career as a labourer lasted a couple of weeks, after which time Dad and I parted professional company by mutual consent. He'd had enough of me skulking around and shirking and I'd had enough of working for him. It wasn't that I thought the work was below me in any way. At that point in my life, I didn't have any professional self-esteem or ambition. It just wasn't for me. The lasting effect the job left on me was that from then on, when someone mentioned the word 'work', I equated it with hard physical graft, dirt and discomfort. And as I had discovered, I was not cut out for that kind of endeavour, therefore I was not cut out for work.

My main interests were going out drinking, causing mischief, hanging out in the local park with my mates, chatting up girls and having what I assumed was fun.

I was a product of my environment, living in an ordinary part of Essex where my peers and I shared a limited view of life, drifting day-to-day without direction.

That was my life at sixteen, which was very different from my life up to ten. Until then, my family – Mum, Dad, two brothers – were wealthy. Dad's building and property development company did well. We lived in a lovely, detached house in South Woodham Ferrers, a wealthy Essex commuter belt town. We had nice holidays, flash cars, and privilege. I went to a private school. My friends all came from well-to-do families. We were part of the wealthy Essex elite, which consisted of self-made businesspeople, sole traders and people who worked in the nearby City of London. It was all going very well until the early nineties when the UK plunged into recession and my family were caught in the financial storm. By that point we had also diversified and owned two transport cafés. One was in Chelmsford and one in Hatfield Peveral. My parents later explained that we were over-leveraged. We had mortgages on all three businesses and the family house. When interest rates started to rocket, the small business empire my family had built fell apart and like many others in the 1990s my dad was forced into bankruptcy. In the pressure my parents split up and everything changed. It all happened within what seemed like the blink of an eye.

Me, Mum and my brothers found ourselves living in a filthy, neglected bungalow behind a workers' café. I vividly remember walking into the bungalow in tears with my mum and brothers, who were also crying. We felt very hard done by because we had been used to so much more. Mum, to her credit, refrained from weeping and worked very hard to make our new accommodation into a home.

The reason we had a roof over our heads at all was because Mum had some help from an accountant who she speaks very fondly of to this day. His name was John Archer and he negotiated with the bank to ensure we could keep the bungalow and run the café with heavily reduced payments. It was the only thing we managed to salvage from the financial ruins.

To make ends meet, Mum got up at five a.m. and worked until three p.m. cooking greasy fry-ups for lorry drivers. She learned how to run the business with no experience. She recruited a team and built the business up on a shoestring budget, working under immense financial pressure and stress, whilst simultaneously raising three children, getting us up, taking us to school and picking us up after. Perhaps she needs to write a book about multi-tasking! My siblings and I were also troublemakers with no respect for authority or rules, which didn't make Mum's life any easier at a time when she was also dealing with the pain of divorce. It wasn't easy for her, and I look back at what she managed to accomplish with a huge amount of respect.

School never held much attraction for me. The only subject I had any interest in was drama. I found lessons unengaging. It's not that I wasn't capable. In later life I pursued knowledge and learning with a rabid thirst, reading book after book. But at school, if you didn't follow the system and learn by rote, you were written off.

Years later I learned that people are either left-brained or right-brained and that learning style depends on which hemisphere of your brain is the more dominant. If the left side of your brain is in the driving seat, it's believed you're mostly analytical and methodical in your thinking. Left-brain thinkers are academic, they're slow-paced and have high levels of attention. The traditional school learning system – memorise, contextualise and regurgitate – favours left-brainers who are better equipped to perform in tests. Left-brain qualities, however, are not the characteristics of entrepreneurial and business success. On the other hand, right-brain people are creative, extrovert, and comfortable with risk. These are the qualities that drive successful businesspeople. I'm a right-brain person and right-brain dominance doesn't fit in at school where the system tries to make every right-brainer into a left-brainer. Instead, the UK education system just creates kids classed as disruptive and problematic because no one knows how to handle them. The frequent irony is that left-brainers pass their exams and excel in the academic environment, but then leave education and struggle in the real world where they've got to make stuff happen, problem-solve and be creative.

After financial ruin and family breakdown forced us from the affluence of the Essex stockbroker belt, we ended up in a place called Hatfield Peverel which, to put it kindly, was different to what we had grown used to. It wasn't inner-city decay by any stretch, there were lots of open green spaces but there was nothing there for young kids to do, especially when you had parents who were primarily concerned with working to earn enough to survive, so we mainly roamed the streets, occasionally asking adults to buy us alcohol in the corner shop.

The funny thing about it all is that when I look back on my childhood now, with all its chaos and lack of direction, I still view it with fondness. I was free, without responsibility and pretty much was left to my own devices, which I loved. I was growing up and living day by day without much thought about the future or where I wanted to be. Success to me back then was earning enough money with as little effort as possible to party at the weekend.

I left school with only one GCSE, a B in Drama. I didn't turn up for most of the other exams and mainly got U grades, which stands for ungraded. I was a nightmare student. One day my art teacher told me with great enthusiasm that the only place I would end up would be prison. Over the years many old classmates have reached out to me on social media expressing genuine shock at what I have been able to accomplish because I acted like a moron and made little to no effort in class. I only tell you this because in many cultures, success is measured on grades and how you perform in education. I want you to know that no matter where you are starting from, you can achieve what you want regardless of how you performed in these environments.

Despite the love and respect I now have for my mum's accomplishments, we had a fractious relationship when I was a teenager and I moved out of home aged 15. My dad had a flat in Hatfield Peveral. He lived with his partner, Jenny, in Terling, a small village not far away. His small flat was empty so I moved in and from the age of 15 was living there mainly on my own, except for when Dad sometimes stayed. This taught me to be independent early in life. I soon realised I needed to make money in order to eat. I took to independent living well and only ever lived with my mum again for a short period when was 25 and I starting my own business. Instead for most of my young adult life, until I could buy a property myself, I rented places with my friends, and mainly with my best friend, James. We rented three places together over the years.

Driven by the need to earn money to survive, I applied for all sorts of jobs without success, mainly because I had no qualifications, no experience, and no idea what I wanted to do. Which is why I ended up working with my dad, who also employed my brothers multiple times. Ultimately, of the three of us only my eldest brother ever took to the family industry.

The only thing my spell as a labourer taught me was that whatever I did subsequently, I didn't want to work in construction. I was sixteen and on the scrapheap. And so, I did what the other people on the scrapheap do, and I started from the bottom. In my case, I went and got a job in a fast-food restaurant.

At the time I had a friend who was working at KFC and who promised that he could get me a job. Having failed to find any alternatives, I took him up on his offer and began work as one of Colonel Sanders' loyal lieutenants, working the fryers, coating the chicken pieces and assembling the Zinger burgers. Did I learn the Colonel's secret recipe? I couldn't possibly tell you. It is a trade secret.

I suppose the big lesson I learned from my parents was work ethic. Even though I wasn't greatly motivated by what I was doing, I knew that once I left school, I had to find a job. But I didn't want to follow in Dad's footsteps—or my brother's, for that matter. He became a bricklayer.

And even though I worked in catering, I knew that wasn't my future either, having watched my mum covered in grease from six in the morning to the late afternoon, running around like a nutter serving people. I knew that I had to work—I just didn't want to do *that* kind of work.

The saving grace of the KFC role, which was hardly a dream job, was that it was much better than labouring and was made bearable, even fun, by the motley crew of Bargain Bucket buccaneers I worked with, led by the manager, who had ways of dealing with drunk, abusive late-night customers that would have made the Colonel spin in his grave.

I ended up working at KFC for a year because it suited my lifestyle at the time, which revolved around going out, getting drunk and generally being a menace. I wasn't bothered about promotion or career progression because it wasn't a career. It was a means to an end. A way to make some money.

After a time, however, I did start to learn a few lessons that would help in later life, particularly about quality and service. I understood that when I cooked the chicken it could come out bad or it could come out well. A good portion of chicken came out of the fryer frothy and evenly coated with that secret mix of eleven herbs and spices. If you went into our KFC branch, or any KFC branch for that matter, the quality of your chicken, and hence the quality of your dining experience, very much depended on the person manning the fryer and dipping the chicken. If I was doing it, you'd get a beautiful, evenly coated box of chicken pieces because I wanted to make good chicken.

If it was someone who didn't care, you'd get a sorry looking pile of legs, wings and ribs. I started to take pride in my work. I wanted people to realise that Adam makes the best chicken, so I took care with what I was doing. I wanted to make the best Twisters and the best fillet burgers. I found out that I was competitive, and I started to understand that if you have to do a job, you might as well do it to the best of your ability, and if you keep practising, you can get good at it. I learned that with time and application, you can achieve things.

But although I was quite content cruising along in the KFC kitchen, head office had other plans and a new management team was brought in to run the place, which subsequently went from being a crazy circus, staffed by reprobates, to a precision-based unit, churning out exact, identikit meals to the hungry Essex post-pub clientele. Those of us who survived the new regime hated the change but with the benefit of hindsight, I can see the bosses did the right thing from a business perspective. However, all the fun died and suddenly, just like school, I no longer fitted in.

During the time I worked at KFC I developed more of a focus and more of an idea of what I wanted to do. From the hot, greasy steam of the deep fryers, I forged an ambition that evolved from my understanding of the type of job I didn't want to do. I realised that if I had to work for the rest of my life, I wanted to work in an office. I didn't know what office, and I didn't have a clue what I would do when I got a job in that office, I just knew I wanted to work in office. And wear a suit. Or, at the very least, smart trousers and a shirt.

Why was I fixated on working in an office? Offices were warm and clean. They were indoors. They didn't smell of fried food. You didn't have to serve drunk people late at night. People in offices were glamorous and exciting. Someone else emptied the bins for you.

But without qualifications or experience, my office dream was just that… a dream. I had no reasonable expectation that I'd ever work in one, that is how low my opinion of myself was at that stage. I didn't even believe I was worthy of a job as an office junior.

Fortuitously, at around the same time as my working relationship with Colonel Sanders was starting to sour, a friend of mine, Andy, began working in an electrical retailers called Powerhouse. When I mentioned my office dream to him one day in the park we hung around in, he said he'd put in a good word for me at Powerhouse.

He was true to his word, and I got an interview, in which I performed hopelessly. It was more challenging than the KFC interview, in which a willingness to work late nights for a low hourly wage seemed to be the main prerequisite for employment. The Powerhouse interviewer asked me difficult questions: What could I bring to the role? Why was I the best person for the job? Where did I see myself in five years?

I heard nothing for a week, but fortune changed when, back at the park, Andy told me he'd been sacked. The following day I received a call offering me his job. Out of loyalty I checked with him first, and he was full of encouragement and told me to accept it, which I did. I couldn't believe my luck. I was employed as a sales assistant in an indoor environment. At the time, for me, that was close to living the dream. It wasn't quite an office, it was a showroom full of TVs, washing machines, cookers, toasters and dishwashers, but for a seventeen-year-old who had previously only shovelled cement and fried chicken, it was a form of paradise. It felt like a different world. It felt professional and grown-up. Everyone who worked there was smartly dressed. They were skilled and confident. It sounds sad, but one of the biggest draws for me was the fact that they had a coffee machine for the staff, and you could have as much coffee as you wanted. The showroom had offices and a lunchroom. There was a place for staff to eat.

Everything was clean and it was full of technology that I couldn't afford.

The salary was around £12,000 a year, which I was more than happy with. But then, on the first day on the job, the manager sat me down and told me something that changed my life.

"So how it works, Adam, is that these people come in, you go and talk to the people, and if they buy a TV, you get a percentage of the ticket price," he explained. "With other items, you get up to five per cent and there are also promotions where you can win vouchers and prizes."

I was confused. I frowned and stopped him. I needed clarification.

"Hang on," I said. "You're telling me that if I talk to people and they buy something, you give me more money?"

He nodded.

"Are you actually serious?" I exclaimed. "I earn more money if I sell this stuff?"

"Of course," he replied. "You go and talk to people, and you ask them questions to find out what they want, what their needs are, and you have to learn about the products."

"And then, if they buy something, I get extra rewards?" I confirmed.

I was genuinely shocked. I assumed that I got paid to deal with customers and that was that. But commission? I'd never even considered that that was part of the package. At that stage I had never worked in a professional environment and was very naïve.

From that day on, everything was different. I was like the Tasmanian devil on that showroom floor. I walked around talking to everybody. As soon as a customer walked through the door, I was the first one there. I was like an attack dog. But a friendly one who knew a lot about televisions.

"Hello sir, what can I help you with today?" I was on it and within a week I was the top salesperson in the store. It was easy, like taking candy from a baby. All you had to do was talk to people. Realising that I had an obvious talent, a lady who worked at the store, Diane, took me under her wing and helped me refine my technique, so I wasn't so blunt. After I'd been there a few weeks, Dad came in and I introduced him to her.

"That boy is the best salesman I've ever seen," she told him. I'm jumping ahead a bit here but later, when I featured on the television show *Rich House Poor House* with my Dad, he mentioned this story and I must admit I smiled with fond memories.

Diane's encouragement was a key motivator, as at that point no-one, no teacher or employer, had ever given me any type of compliment and encouragement. The influence Diane had on me at that key point in my life was huge. A little encouragement here and there is so important, and I am grateful to her to this day.

I started earning more money. I became one of the best salespeople in the group. If there was a promotion on a certain TV one week that earned me an extra few per cent in commission, every customer I spoke to that week was buying one of those TVs. There was also a competition to win your own large screen TV, which I wanted badly and which I won. That giant TV that took pride of place in my tiny little bedroom. I was like a man possessed. I had found my calling.

At Powerhouse I learned the power of focus. I set goals and targets in my head and worked towards them. Reaching them and exceeding them gave me an incredible feeling. Deciding what you want in life, working towards making it happen and then accomplishing it really does build your confidence, even if you start small and win a TV. The key is the power of focus and the work ethic to make it happen.

It is too easy to say I was motivated by the money because underneath there was something else driving me. The success.

For the first time in my life, I understood what success felt like. Before that I felt like life was off-limits to me and that I couldn't have anything. Now I realised I could have anything I wanted if I had the right strategies to get it.

Success was like a drug, and I became addicted.

MILLIONAIRE
SUCCESS SECRETS

- Set clear goals, even if you're uncertain about the path to reach them!
- Never let your circumstances define you; instead, empower yourself to become the person you aspire to be.
- Academic success should not be the sole focus of your journey. Embrace your talents and strengths.
- Cultivate a Strong Work Ethic and Embrace the Power of Diligence
- Embrace a strong sense of pride and passion in everything you do, no matter the task or project.
- Conversations create opportunity.
- Embrace the feeling of success, regardless of the path that led you there. You deserve it.

2

Why Me? And Why You Should Listen to What I Say

S o why am I telling you this and, more importantly, what makes a former Powerhouse Employee of the Month qualified to write a book about success?

Well, those early successes in the home entertainment aisle set me on a journey that resulted in me becoming one of the UK's most successful young entrepreneurs of his generation. I've been on the success journey and on the way, I've learned and analysed the strategies needed to achieve success—not just in business but in all walks of life, relationships, health, and personal growth. I was a millionaire before I reached the age of thirty. I started businesses from scratch and grew them in rapid time to become wildly successful. I've employed up to 120 people at a time, presided over a business with a turnover of more than £40m a year and have helped others achieve their dreams too.

I was a pioneer of social media marketing. My first successful business featured heavily in the media and was in the 100 Businesses to Inspire Britain list three years running. The London Stock Exchange talked about how I'd sold £50m worth of vehicles through social media marketing. I built the largest social media following in the automotive industry and the rest of the industry had no idea the opportunity existed.

My coaching and wealth-creation business, Big Business Events, creates millionaires and helps businesses develop into successful money-making machines.

I've mentored hundreds of people to be the best versions of themselves. I've taken businesses from £100,000 annual turnover to £3m annual turnover in just a year. I've given them the strategies, marketing skills, sales expertise and practical knowledge to be the best in their sectors. I've created Young Entrepreneurs of the Year. I've taken an Uber driver and given him the coaching and skills that enabled him to become a property millionaire. Another client started out with me when he was running a business drawing plans for other people's houses, now he earns so much that he's recently built his own 12,000sqft dream mansion.

If you want more credentials, look at my lifestyle. I live in a mansion on the most expensive road in Essex and I drive a Bentley. I've had Ferraris and Lamborghinis. I've lived the five-star VIP lifestyle. I've kept company with some of the biggest global icons from show business, sport and commerce. I've shared stages with John Travolta, Al Pacino, Calvin Klein and Floyd Mayweather. I've shared my success secrets with audiences of thousands.

But I've also learned hard lessons. I know that the cars, the big houses and the holidays mean nothing if you haven't got authenticity, empathy, and substance. I've come very close to losing it all and rebuilt myself even stronger. Failure and humility are important aspects of success and I have tasted them many times.

Today, as one of the world's top Business Coaches, I share what I've learned on my journey. I help people to become more successful. I'm a Business and Wealth coach unlike any other. I show people the strategies of success, which you will find throughout this book. I share the lessons I have learned along the way, which if adopted can make a life-changing impact. I teach people exactly like you, how to grow and develop and how to make more money if that's what they want to do. With my events company, Big Business Events, I host seminars and conferences in which audiences learn the secrets of personal and business growth. I personally coach and mentor individuals on my Business Circle, Gold Circle and Inner Circle programmes and help them to achieve their dreams. I've been super-successful, turning countless entrepreneurs into bona fide business titans.

And it's not all about the money, although for most people money does create a path to happiness. I've helped people find their passion and way in life. I've given them the tools needed to lead more focused and meaningful lives.

The secret of success lies in my plans, which are simple and easy to follow yet incredibly powerful. I'll give you these in detail in this book. These formulas are simple and effective and easy to use in every aspect of your life.

Want to become a millionaire? Want to become successful in business? Want to become a better husband, wife, or partner? This book is here to arm you with the tools you need to create success in your life, however you define it.

I am an expert at showing people how to harness the skills required for success. In my work as a coach, this enables my clients to build businesses, increase turnover and make more money. I can take anyone and give them the tools, ideas, and strategies they need to be a success in whatever endeavour they choose, to build their brands and to excel in life. It doesn't matter who you are. If you want to develop your skills grow and succeed, no matter where you are starting from, the simple principles and systems we use can take you there.

MILLIONAIRE
SUCCESS SECRETS

- Don't be shy about sharing your successes, if you don't share your wins, no one else will.
- Let people know why you are the best person for the job.
- Learn from those with expertise and with valid credentials.
- Only take advice from those you would swap places with.

3

What Is Success? – Delving Deeper into the Elements that Create Successful Lives

What do we mean by success? For each individual, the answer will be slightly different. For some people, success is money; for others, it's about recognition. When I was sitting on that staircase many years ago picking flecks of rubble from the carpet, success for me would have been a warm office job. As I got older, my horizons changed, and my idea of success became money and status. Our ideas about success change as we grow because we experience different things and our values and priorities change.

Success for me now is also about being a good father to my son, and about helping others achieve success for themselves. Success also exists on a continuum. When you obtain success in one aspect of your life, often you reset your expectations and strive for another level of success.

This idea is best illustrated in a psychological theory commonly known as Maslow's hierarchy of needs. Abraham Maslow was an American psychologist who created a model of psychological health based on fulfilling innate human needs in order of priority. His model was published in a 1943 paper and is commonly represented in a triangular diagram, divided into between five and eight horizontal sections, depending on whether you are looking at the advanced or simplified version. The bottom tiers are classed as basic needs and include food, water, safety and security. The next level is classified as 'belonging and love' and includes intimate relationships and friends. The level above this is esteem, which includes prestige and feelings of accomplishment. These base levels are classed as psychological needs. The top level is classed as 'self-actualisation', which is defined as achieving one's full potential. Creative activities are included at this level. Maslow theorised that once lower-level needs are realised, higher-level needs become more of a priority.

The ideas of success that we develop throughout our lifetime can mirror this hierarchy, to a degree. For example, when we start out in business, survival and security in the form of financial success are key needs. Once we achieve these, we generally do not stop taking measures to ensure these needs are met but we may also move on to look for other successes, perhaps striving to win plaudits in a chosen profession by trying to win awards. In Maslow's model, this would constitute a desire to fulfil psychological needs.

Achieving success is much easier when you know what success looks like. This is why the first step on the road to success is defining what you want your success to be, and then visualising that.

For example, when I set my focus on being a better parent to my son, I asked myself: 'what does a better dad look like?' When I considered the question, I realised that it didn't necessarily mean trying to win a 'Dad of the Year' award. The key elements to my idea of parental success were that I spend time with my son, engage with him when we are together, be there for him, support him and ensure that he feels secure and happy. Success to me means developing a closer bond with my son so he loves spending time with me.

Once I established those goals I could work backwards, putting in place the strategies and changes in my life needed to achieve the overall goal – or success.

This strategy works for everything. You want to have a successful garden? What does a successful garden look like? What are the elements of a successful garden? Once you've worked that out, work back from there, addressing each element until you achieve your successful garden. The key is to define and then segment. And then when you have attained success in the areas you want to be successful in, you can identify other areas of your life in which to use the strategy.

It helps if you are honest with yourself. For example, there are areas in my life that I'm not as successful in as I would like.

I know that over the years at times I have put on a few pounds and my fitness is not as good as it could be and that I need to improve it. We get what we focus on, and focus is one of the key lessons in success. When you lose focus in an area, it invariably suffers. More recently I wanted to commit to improving my fitness. I defined what I envisaged success in this area to be. This is an important step because until you understand what your definition of success is, you have no target, at best a moving target.

For me it was clear. I didn't want a six-pack or to look super-ripped and pumped. That was a journey I didn't want to go on. I simply wanted to increase my energy levels so I could perform better in my speaking and presentations.

That was my goal, and I then segmented that goal into the steps I needed to take to get there. I spoke to a coach, mentor and friend who is full of energy, and who I respect greatly, Sarah

Willingham, a former Dragon from the TV show Dragons Den. I asked her what she does to boost her energy levels. She suggested I purchased an Apple Watch and use the Apple fitness app to help me focus on the daily KPIs I needed to achieve to reach my goal. I got an exercise plan that fitted into my life without affecting success in other areas. The result was that in a very short period I was able to monitor and measure my fitness and energy levels and lose over one and half stone while feeling more energetic.

Success is a journey, both in terms of how your definitions of success change through life and in terms of the steps you must take to achieve success. Anyone can be successful at the end of the journey. The key is that, in order to be endpoint successful, you need to start the journey. And the journey is a commitment that you make to yourself where you make a pledge to achieve whatever success you are pursuing.

The journey starts when you say to yourself: 'Right! This is what I want to do, and this is where I want to go.'

If you make that commitment to yourself, and if you are willing to do whatever it takes to get to that end point, then you will succeed. No question about it.

There is a disclaimer, however. You must put in the effort to get what you want and to reach your success destination.

There is a school of thought that says if you want something hard enough, and if you visualise it enough, the universe will deliver it to you. Unfortunately, that's not how it works in the real world. You need to know what you want, and you need to commit to attaining it, but then you must take action to achieve it. You need to work at it.

Inevitably, as you pursue success, you will encounter others who tell you that you can't do it, or that it's too hard and maybe you need to lower your expectations. Often these people are motivated by jealousy or are aware of their own failings and want to see them in others to feel better about themselves. You can choose to listen to these people, or you can choose to listen to yourself. I know that if I listened to all the negative voices and the naysayers who scoffed when I told them I was going to be a millionaire by the age of thirty, I may not have made the decisions I did that led me on my path to success. If you choose to listen to yourself, you become the driver of your own persistence.

By reading this book you are on your way because you have the right information, which is contained in these pages. This will allow you to act. By ignoring the negative voices, you begin to create the right environment and by committing to your achievements, you will become persistent.

And this is one of the key lessons I want you to know. The four stages of success are information, action, environment, and persistence.

Here's why these four stages work so well. Want to be a good pilot? First, you need to get the right information. Where is the best place to learn? What's the process? What is the cost? Who's the best instructor? Once you have the information you need, you then take action. Book lessons. Next, create the right environment. Go to the airfield. Finally, be persistent. Take as many lessons as you need and practise, practise, practise.

How about relationships? Want to have a successful relationship? Get the information. What does a successful relationship look like? How should people in relationships treat each other? Once you've worked that out, put it in action. Do the things you've learned. Create a supportive environment for that relationship. Spend time with couples who are in successful relationships. And be persistent. Continue to develop and grow that relationship because if you become complacent, relationships soon stop developing.

Throughout this book there are many lessons that will help you develop your success in every area of your life, one of the most powerful frameworks I use is this simple four-stage strategy (which I'll develop as we progress through these pages). The more you use this strategy, the easier you'll find it is to be a success.

MILLIONAIRE
SUCCESS SECRETS

- Success is a journey that doesn't depend on where you begin. Start by fulfilling your basic needs, and gradually expand your vision, one step at a time.
- Clarify your personal definition of success and what it looks like. Break down the key components and actions required to reach your vision.
- Ground your aspirations in reality; setting achievable goals, both short-term and long-term, is the first step to success.
- Notice the difference between constructive criticism and jealousy. Embrace constructive criticism and move on.
- The 4 elements of success are:
  1. Specialised information
  2. Take action
  3. Environment
  4. Persistence

4

Foundations – What Are the Starting Points of My Success?

I n earlier chapters, I mentioned we owned two transport cafés and a construction and property business, and we lived in some beautiful homes in the quaint villages of Essex. The school I attended was so posh I wore a little cap and carried a satchel.

And then in the early 1990s, there was a recession. It hit homeowners and people with property investments particularly hard. During the recession interest rates shot up and for a while reached 15%. Like many others, my dad couldn't keep up with his repayments and lost it all.

Everything changed. I was pulled out of private school and enrolled in the local comprehensive. The first day I turned up, I was wearing my private-school cap and carrying my satchel. I soon learned that wasn't a great look if I wanted to fit in and make friends. I went through a full transition within a week and ended up looking like all the other children, with scuffed shoes, shirt untucked, tie hanging halfway down my chest.

When we had to move out of the house, I felt like my whole world had fallen apart. We went from living in a beautiful house to a bungalow at the back of a transport café. The house was horrific. It was tiny and had been neglected. There was nothing in it and I remember going in there with my mum and brothers and looking around in shock.

I'm not one for resentfulness or dwelling on negatives, but at that age, I imagine I probably was resentful at the hand life had dealt me and my family.

Now, I know I was a bit older than eight years old, but that experience probably did leave some sort of psychological mark on me. Because maybe it's harder to have something and then lose it than to never have it at all. Do you want it more if you've had it and lost it? I think maybe you do because you can't miss what you never had.

In the years that followed, I was undoubtedly an angry teenager. I was rebellious and feral. I gained nothing from school except maybe the ability to be sociable. Maybe it was something to do with that formative experience, which I also believe put drive in me. I'd had everything, and I'd had nothing, and I knew which one I preferred.

Perhaps that was the reason why, when I started to excel at selling electrical goods in Powerhouse, a little light went on inside me. The success I started to achieve, through action and persistence, showed me that I was in control of my fate. For the first time in my life I was able to afford what I couldn't have before, and I started to earn good money. My basic needs were met and then I started to prioritise my psychological needs. I won accolades and I became confident in my ability.

So much so that when the senior salesman left, I applied for his job and got it. The position came with a much higher basic salary and more privileges, and I was up against a colleague who had been there for several years and had more experience. Most of the staff there assumed the older, more experienced candidate would get the job, but the bosses could see my potential. I was the top performing salesman week after week. The promotion was one of the first successes that I'd ever experienced and was made even sweeter because it was against expectations. A few months later, I won a nationwide competition for commission earned per hour.

The retail group had 230 stores and I was becoming the best salesman in them all. I went to a glitzy award ceremony and was invited on stage to get my trophy. I was nineteen. For such a young kid, it was an amazing experience and helped galvanise my mind into thinking about what was possible in life. I had a new persona, a new identity. I was a successful salesman. I was more confident. I talked differently. I acted differently. I was a different person.

While I placed myself in the environment of the Powerhouse sales team hall of fame, I also had another environment, which was my group of friends in Chelmsford. This environment involved going out drinking as many times a week as I possibly could, spending the money I was earning. One of the girls in this group got a new boyfriend who everyone spoke very highly of. He was creating success in his life and seemed to have it worked out. With my new identity of believing I was the best salesperson out there I was of course curious to meet him. He rocked up to pick up his girlfriend in a brand new Chrysler and was smart as a whip.

He was only a few years older than me, and we got talking.

"What do you do?" I asked.

"I'm a car dealer," he said, adding that he worked for Chrysler and that the car was supplied through the dealership he worked at.

"Does it pay well?" I enquired.

"I'm on £50,000 a year," he answered.

I think my mouth fell open at that point. I didn't believe it was possible to earn that sort of money selling cars. I was earning around £35,000 and I thought I was doing very well.

I've got to be in car sales, I thought to myself.

Ironically, a few years previously when I was working for my dad, we were renovating a house near a small car dealership. One day when we passed it, Dad suggested I should think about getting into the motor trade. He even took me in to talk to the owner.

"Everyone who sells cars earns money," he said. "You'd be good at it."

At the time I assumed he was just keen to offload me onto someone else.

But now, thanks to Mr Chrysler, I was beginning to see the possibilities. Not only was the money good, but you also got a company car.

I started looking for jobs in car sales and, still aged just nineteen, applied for one at a local Ford dealership, which was holding a recruitment day.

I went along to find seventy-five people of all ages and abilities hoping to get chosen for the two positions on offer. I was the youngest there by a mile. There was one other notable young person, a man named James who was a Brentwood boy. He was smartly dressed in a striped shirt and had combed-back hair with blond highlights. He was clearly sharp as hell and had been working in London as a stockbroker.

The day was set up as a series of heats. If you passed one, you went through to the next round until the field was whittled down to the final two successful candidates. It was a brutal way of choosing staff.

In the first challenge, the applicants were sectioned into groups and were given tasks. The group I was in were asked to sit around a table. There was a whiteboard next to the table with a list of random objects written on it. An assessor was assigned to each group and the one assigned to mine explained: "You're going to live on a desert island and there's a list of things on the whiteboard that you can take with you. Working as a team, I want you to decide what you are going to take and why."

I realise now the task was about finding out who had initiative, who could solve problems, who was leadership material and who had communication skills. Everyone started talking. I sat there silently. I was non-existent in the conversation and soon realised that if I was to stand any chance of getting the job, I needed to be noticed, so I stood up, got a pen, walked over to the board, and started controlling the conversation and the group.

"OK, everybody, so what do we need to take?" I asked.

Everyone looked at me as if to say, who the hell is this kid? But I carried on and guided the group to make decisions. After about fifteen minutes, we all reconvened again and, after some deliberation in one of the offices, one of the people in charge came out with a list of names which he read. He asked those who were on the list to go and stand on the other side of the room. There were only around fifteen names on the list. James and I were called. Those whose names had not been called were thanked and told they had not been successful. The rest of us were told we were through to the next stage and that we were going to give individual talks to the panel about our most successful achievement. It was explained that each of us would have five minutes to impress the judges.

I was genuinely surprised I'd made it through the first round.

When it was my turn, I talked about my success at Powerhouse, about winning the most commission per hour in my job and about being the top salesman in the company. I could see that the panel were all engaged, and I remember thinking, *I can't even believe that they're interested.* At the end of the five minutes, I thanked them for listening and turned to leave the room.

"Whoa!" one of them said. "Where are you going?"

I didn't realise they were going to question me as well.

The next five minutes consisted of rapid-fire questions.

"How old are you?"

"Where are you from?"

"What are your ambitions?"

"What would you say are your key qualities?"

When it was over, I went back outside and watched the other applicants file in and out, thinking to myself that there was no way I'd get the job because they were all older, smarter and more experienced. Of course, this was an incredibly negative mindset to have. At the time I didn't realise that. I was simply overwhelmed by the environment. But since then I learned that another key to success is self-belief and how you see and value yourself, regardless of who you are speaking to. Whoever you speak to, wherever you are, believing in your own value is a critical area of success. If you suffer from low self-esteem and low self-worth, you will need to work on this in order to be successful in your life.

Back to the Ford showroom where another five applicants were thanked and sent away, having been unsuccessful. At that stage I started to develop a small bit of self-belief. Maybe, just maybe, I was going to get the job.

The final stage was a proper interview. I was asked lots more questions. When it was over, I was thanked, and they explained that they would be in touch.

I felt deflated. I thought after all the effort we'd made they'd make their choices there and then. As I left, I assumed that was the last I'd hear. I went back to Powerhouse and put it to the back of mind.

But two days later I got a call from one of the men who had been on the interview panel. He explained that he wanted to see me for another interview. I went to the showroom in Romford and the manager met me and invited me into his office where I was joined by two of the management team and grilled with questions. Despite being nervous, I stood up to the challenge and battled hard. I sensed I was close to success. But then they hit me with a huge objection which was hard to hear.

"Look," it was explained, "we want to offer you the job because we think you can do it, but we have never had anyone as young as you in this position. You get a company car, and we can't even get you insured because of your age, so we've got a few challenges, and perhaps we will need to invite you back when you are 21."

That was two years away. In this pivotal moment I could have deflated and sulked, however the instincts I had developed at Powerhouse from dealing with so many people daily told me they wanted me to convince them. So my confidence kicked into gear, knowing the deal was close.

"I know I can do this and I am more than capable and if you give me the opportunity you will not regret it," I pushed.

Their serious looks broke into smiles. It was a test. They wanted to see if I could hold my own and they wanted to find out how I reacted when I was told no, or not now.

They said they needed a quick discussion in private and left me in the room alone for what felt like an eternity. I badly wanted that job. I felt it was the one big opportunity I had to get into the big time, because at that stage I really didn't have a lot. I lived in a tiny flat, I was barely able to make the rent, money was tight and my car was falling apart.

The carrot they were dangling in front of me was a company car, an opportunity to earn £50,000 a year and the status of working in a beautiful showroom surrounded by nice new cars and with top, super-smart people.

They came back and told me they could make some amendments to their insurance policy and offered me the job.

I was thrilled and started as soon as I'd worked my notice at Powerhouse. It didn't even matter that they gave me the worst car you've ever seen, a Ford Fusion Durashift, in Oyster Brown. It really was horrendous, but for me I felt like I had moved up in the world because it was brand new, and I'd never had a brand-new car before. I was nineteen and I felt like the king of the world.

On my first day in the job, I learned that the other younger candidate, James, had also been successful and we started together as the newbies.

After Powerhouse, Ford in Romford, Essex was a baptism of fire. It was the most competitive environment you've ever seen.

There were ten people in sales, and we all sat in a row by reception. Customers walked in and the receptionist would then call one of us over to meet the client and we would take them back to the desk and start the enquiry process. There were two ways of meeting clients: if you were available and everyone else was busy or if the receptionist liked you. I realised very quickly that it was important to make friends with her and looked for excuses to hang around the reception desk.

The other way to pick up sales was via phone-ins. In the middle of the row of sales seats, there was a small table on which sat the MarTech phone. Phone enquiries from adverts in newspapers and magazines were forwarded to the MarTech phone. It was like the Bat Phone. When it rang, someone was on the other end of the line who wanted to ask about buying a car, and sales assistants would run from all angles trying to get to it first.

It was a hardcore sales environment. To make money you had to be at the top of your game. And with only around £30-£100 commission for each car sold, you had to sell a lot of cars to make a good wage.

I was still leading a questionable lifestyle, going out several nights a week, drinking and partying, and it was just not going to wash with the bosses, who demanded high standards and hard work. Within the first couple of weeks, I realised just how strict the culture was when I turned up late and worse for wear after a particularly lively night out. I was bleary-eyed and unshaven and when I walked into the morning sales meeting, the manager gave me both barrels.

"Look at the state of you. You haven't shaved. Go home. I don't want you in my showroom!" he yelled.

I stuttered, "W-w-what do you mean? I've driven an hour."

"Go home now," he ordered.

I was shocked and skulked off home.

The next day, when he'd calmed down, I was called into his office.

"Never come to my f**king showroom looking like that again," he growled.

I never did.

The environment was hard, it was focused on sales and hard work. You were expected to be disciplined and I was not used to it. There was also a strange mentality toward new people coming in and in hindsight it was not a supportive environment for a young newbie looking to learn the ropes. It was sink or swim and there were massive expectations on staff. If you didn't cut it you were out.

In the first week I was read the rules, by one of the favoured members of the sales team, Lisa,

"You're New Boy; you don't have a name until you ain't New Boy anymore, which will be when we bring in someone else new," I was told.

This missive was delivered playfully but she meant it and everyone in the sales team called me New Boy for the first six months. Other more spiteful members of the sales team took great pleasure in telling me that 'no one survives'. They had little faith in me because I was so young. I lost count of the times various members of the sales team told me 'you won't get by here, you haven't got what it takes'.

But I could see from the others that once you were established, you were left alone. Until you proved yourself, however, you were under immense pressure and had to earn your respect, which was tough.

As part of the targets, I had to make and answer a certain number of calls each day. I was set daily KPIs and was not allowed to go home until I'd achieved them. The managers listened in on my calls through connected phones in their offices and regularly called me in to pull apart my sales technique.

There was a lot to keep up with, and I had the added challenge of having to fill out paperwork. There was a lot of it, and I was terribly disorganised. I'd never had to do admin before. At Powerhouse there wasn't a great deal of paperwork involved in selling a TV or a washing machine. But car sales were different. There was finance to arrange, part-exchange details to deal with, and registration documents to see to. I understood sales, but I didn't understand the paperwork.

I soon learned that my old Tasmanian devil method of trying to speak to everyone in the showroom and closing the sale as quickly as possible just didn't work in car sales.

"You need to build a relationship and rapport with the customer," the boss told me.

The process was completely controlled. As a salesman, you met the customer. You talked to the customer and built a relationship. You viewed the car they brought in for part-exchange. You took the details of the part-exchange vehicle to your manager who would then give you a price for it. And from then you talked about the new car they wanted and worked out the best finance model. The part-exchange deal was always agreed on first. I used to whiz through that section to try to make the sale as fast as I could so I could earn my £30-£100 commission and get to the next customer.

The managers realised this was happening and devised a plan. I was told that none of them would give me a part-exchange price until I found out certain details from the customer, such as where they went on holiday, what their names were, if they had children and what they did for a living. Only then, once I'd slowed down and developed a rapport, would I get a part-exchange price and be able to go on to the next step of the process.

The tough love worked, and I became adept at building relationships with clients. Very quickly I went from being New Boy to working up the ranks and competing with the big hitters of the showroom, Brad and Terry, who to this day I love to bits but who at the time were big competition.

They sat next to me on 'sales row' and were slick operators. Terry had several years' experience under this belt and Brad had worked in insurance, so he understood the paperwork and was also great with people. Both would eventually go on to work for me as managers in my business. Another one of the managers at Ford became a finance manager at another of my businesses. I ended up employing a lot of people I worked with on the way up.

But at that stage I was New Boy sitting in the middle of these two older men who helped teach me and became two of the many role models whom I learned from.

Even though the environment was driven, even though I was the junior to begin with, I started to fit in and started to learn and grow.

I started to storm up the sales league table and picked up many plaudits on the way. The company ran national competitions for top performers in which the prize was a place on a company holiday. If you were one of the top sales staff, you'd win a place on the holiday. I went on several of them.

I grew and matured when I was there. One of the managers took me aside one day and told me that I should buy a house and get a mortgage. At the time I was renting a very small flat. Looking back, I think it was his way of trying to get me on the straight and narrow because I was still prone to wild partying. He was encouraging me to grow up and become more responsible. I took his advice and, with a monthly mortgage to service, plus all the other bills that come with owning your own home, I had less disposable income to waste on nights out.

I felt I found a home at Ford. My colleagues were like a family, and I loved it. Eventually, new people were employed, and I was no longer New Boy. And knowing how tough it could be, I helped them.

The management continued to drive me hard and, if I'm honest, I resented the way I felt I was being treated sometimes. I was a high-performing member of the team and felt often that I should have been cut some slack. I put in the hours. I stayed late catching up on calls and took to the role with a commitment like nothing I had ever done before, I grew and grew and eventually I was top of the sales charts on a consistent basis.

Despite it being very hard at times, I am tremendously grateful for the discipline the management there installed in me. When I joined, I was a cocky teenager and over the years I spent there I developed into a focused, disciplined machine. That was down to the many lessons I learned and the solid training I received.

Sales fascinated me and I knew I was good at it, so I started to find out how I could be better. I studied sales techniques. I became fixated with books about sales, psychology and entrepreneurs. I gradually began to wonder if there was enough scope for me in the role. Those above me were doing well, but through books and learning I started to develop larger goals and targets in my mind.

Aged 21, I decided to set myself the goal of being a millionaire before the age of 30. My mind had expanded, my confidence was growing, and I felt I could achieve it. Of course, I didn't know how

I was going to do it, but I was pretty confident selling Ford Fiestas for £30 a pop wouldn't get me there.

At this stage I want to mention that when you get focused, make decisions, and start to forge your own path, there are going to be people around you that feel threatened or don't like this. Later, one of my coaches explained to me: "First, they laugh at you. Second, they think you're crazy. Third they ridicule you for being crazy. Fourth they doubt you. Fifth they wonder if you can. Sixth they respect you. Seventh they tell everyone they always knew you would do it."

The reason I mention this here is because around this stage of my life, when I'd set that goal, one of my brothers and his friend found a diary I had written with all my goals in it and they wound me up relentlessly about what I wanted to achieve, telling me I never would.

Even though Brad and Terry were friends, they also smirked when I told them I wanted to be a millionaire. Today I consider them close friends and they have both gone on to do very well, but even they doubted me. I want you to know that whatever you can perceive in your mind you can achieve regardless of what anyone else tells you if you work towards it with enthusiasm and overcome the hurdles that present themselves. If people doubt you, use it as fuel to drive you even more, because what you see in your mind eventually you can hold in your hand.

Regardless of what was going on around me I knew I could achieve more, and Ford was not giving me the chance to progress at the rate I knew I was capable of. Indeed, the management often referred to how young I was and how lucky I was to be earning great money and driving a new car. It was frequently pointed out that my colleagues were all more than ten years older than me. I wanted more though and after three years, I started to realise it was time for a change.

One of the books I read that impressed me was Sir Alan Sugar's biography. *I've got to work for this man,* I thought to myself.

Fortuitously, I saw an ad for a salesperson in one of Sir Alan's companies, Amsair, which was a private aviation charter company. I applied and got the job. I handed in my notice at Ford and at the exit interview I was strangely overcome with emotion. I burst into tears, this really is unlike me but I think I felt such a deep sense of gratitude to many people there, mixed with the fact I loved working there. The only reason I was leaving was because of my ambition but I couldn't tell the interviewer because anyone I told about my millionaire goal thought I was crazy. They just laughed or told me I couldn't do it. I didn't have the heart to tell him that part of the reason that I was leaving is because I wanted more than they could offer. They all were so sold on the idea that the way they did thing things was the only way. But I knew there was more out there for me.

On the one hand, I resented the role because although I loved it, I had hit the ceiling. I had a lot of respect for the job and understood how much I'd learned there.

I was not unhappy. I loved the team, but I knew I was worth more and was frustrated that although the job had helped me to get to a new stage and a new level in my life, it was not going to take me any further. And I didn't want to stop at that level.

At the exit interview I was told: "Adam, we will always have you back." I appreciated that, but I was leaving because I wanted to go forward so despite the kind offer, I knew when I went that was the end of that chapter.

Despite my enthusiasm when I started at Amsair, my career as the next 'Apprentice' at Alan Sugar's side was very short-lived.

The job wasn't what I thought. I met Sir Alan briefly a few times and never had a conversation with him. I worked with his son Daniel, whom I respected and liked. The job involved leasing private aeroplanes. There were no leads, there were no enquiries. Salespeople had to create their own enquiries and do their own leases. I had taken almost a 50% pay cut to go there and I felt after a few weeks that I'd gone backwards. There was little opportunity, as far as I could see. I was with the company for a few months during which I landed a big deal with Honda, leasing private flights for their CEOs, but it wasn't the money I thought I'd make, and I realised that I'd taken a wrong turn.

I was very frustrated at that point because the last few moves in my career had been successful. I was getting used to winning and the Amsair job was not a win. Those who knew my ambitions had told me it wouldn't work out and it was a little bit embarrassing for that to be coming true. I contemplated staying out of pride, but I wasn't happy, and I couldn't see the role getting me to where I needed to be.

One invaluable lesson I learned, which later proved beneficial when I started my first business, was cold prospecting: the art of creating opportunities from scratch.

I could have gone back to Ford, but I wasn't going to give up on striving for the next level. Before I left Ford, I'd gone for an interview at a BMW showroom and had been offered the job there based on my track record. But I'd turned it down because I was eager to work for Sir Alan. Realising my mistake, I called BMW up and asked if there were any vacancies. The manager remembered me and called me in for a chat. Within a week, I was offered a sales job there, and so I went back into car sales, this time under the tutelage of the German marque.

MILLIONAIRE
SUCCESS SECRETS

- Be curious by acknowledging others' successes and ask insightful questions. If they can achieve it, so can you.
- Don't blend in, STAND OUT. You don't get the opportunities you deserve, you the opportunities you take.
- Discipline is critical to all success – where can you be better?
- Embrace the journey from the ground up; hard work is the foundation of success.

5

People Power – How the People Around You Influence Your Success

Your success is built on the shoulders of those whom you choose to learn from, partner with, and associate with on your journey. You can't achieve success in isolation. There is always input from other people, whether that is as a result of you consciously seeking out experts for advice and the right information, or of you surrounding yourself with inspirational people and creating a nurturing environment in which success can thrive.

We pick up attitudes, ideas, and characteristics from the people around us without even realising it, as if by osmosis. We absorb, assimilate, and instinctively mirror behaviours. We adopt mindsets that we understand to be beneficial.

For example, I was certainly influenced by my mum's work ethic. I saw how hard she worked in the transport café after she and my dad split up, and although I wasn't even aware of it at the time, her actions would have impressed on me the idea that to raise yourself in life, you need to put in the effort. I look back now and marvel at how she managed to work long, hard days and still raise three children. And she wasn't just doing the cooking. She was running the whole show. She was managing and recruiting staff, doing the books, controlling the stock, buying the food. Today she's laid back, but back then she seemed permanently stressed.

With hindsight, I can see why. Running your own business, any kind of business requires dedication and focus.

I learned lessons from my dad too. He taught me about property and has always been there to listen and help when I needed him.

When I look back, I can trace a thread of people who, throughout my life, have had an impact, or who have provided a key lesson at a pivotal time. From my parents to Diane at Powerhouse who believed in my ability, which in turn fuelled my self-belief and made me drive myself to be better.

Diane particularly was a positive force. She was great at sales herself and she taught me that I had to learn about the product. This is a lesson that all salespeople should learn. And all businesspeople for that matter, whether you are selling a toaster, selling a service, selling an idea, or selling yourself. If you don't understand what it is you are selling, and can't explain it to other people, how will anyone else understand?

At Ford, one of the managers had an equally big impact on me. Our relationship was strained at times, however the lessons he taught me in discipline and work ethic are still ingrained in me to this day. He most definitely kept me at arm's length and gave other people opportunities that I never got. Other team members would get to go and play golf with him, I felt very much on the outside of the circle. But what I know now that I didn't know then is that he was the one who polished the diamond. He was the one who found a way of getting the bad habits out of me. He made me change environments and turn my back on the drinking and partying to concentrate on becoming a rounded professional. He moulded me into someone who could cope with the admin and paperwork, and who was capable of building relationships. He made me serious about sales and helped me understand that success in sales wasn't just about trying to turn around as many transactions as possible. He made me realise sales was a much more nuanced game than that.

There were other people at Ford who helped shaped the person I became. The company engaged the services of a trainer from MarTech who came in, sat down and listened through every phone call with me, telling me what I was doing wrong and giving me systems, processes and skills that I still sometimes use today. Because of all these people, within a year of starting the job at Ford, I was earning in excess of £50,000 a year at a very young age and able to go and purchase my first home.

The point I'm trying to get across is that we don't get to where we are in life without input from other people. They create the environment. An environment isn't solely about buildings or locations, it's about the people you choose to be around. Everything I life will come from other people.

Later in life, I met another person who influenced me in many ways. I know her as Gemma, you'll know her as The GC, or Gemma Collins, the superstar from the reality TV show *The Only Way Is Essex*, or TOWIE for short. Gemma was a colleague and then a protégée of mine when I eventually went to work at BMW. She was given to me to train, and we became great friends. She was focused on making money and was superb at relationship building. I helped her hone her selling technique and she provided me with advice about lifestyle and personal matters. She became my lifestyle guru. I could go to her for advice about girlfriends and she told me the best places to go on holiday, what clothes to buy, which aftershave to use, where to eat, the best bars and restaurants.

She said to me: "Adam, you should go to New York." So, I went to New York one year and Gemma practically devised the itinerary for me. She said: "Adam, you should eat at Smiths," so I went and ate at Smiths. I was like her little project. I started experiencing things that I'd never experienced before. She lived a millionaire lifestyle even though she didn't have a million pounds.

We would discuss our ambitions. I told her I wanted to be a millionaire and she told me she wanted to be a star. Other people scoffed, but it was good to be around someone who was as wildly ambitious as I was. There weren't too many people like that in the social circles I moved in.

Gemma and I encouraged each other. I remember her sitting at reception before she trained in sales and she said: "Adam, I'm not going to do this forever."

"What are you going to do?" I asked.

"I'm going to be famous."

She used to say it all the time.

All these experiences and interactions formed an environment in which success manifested itself. They created a narrative in my mind that reaffirmed my belief that I was successful and could be even more successful.

We tell ourselves stories about ourselves and these stories create our self-beliefs. If we are in negative environments surrounded by negative people, we will inevitably tell ourselves negative stories about ourselves. We become programmed to think limiting thoughts.

A technique to help from falling into this trap is to be aware of the language you use, both in your internal dialogue, and externally when you talk about yourself. If you use repetition of positive language, you can programme yourself into believing positive things about yourself.

For example, when you are faced with something and you say or think: 'I can't do this', train your brain to believe you can by repeatedly thinking, 'I *know* I can do this, I *must* do this, I *will* do this'. Positive repetition reinforces positive action. Self-belief creates affirmative action. It starts in the mind; therefore, success starts in the mind.

I witnessed a great example of how environment and the people in it affect mindset recently at one of my Gold Circle mastermind classes. I noticed that one of the attendees, who sometimes could be prone to negative language, was sitting between two of my star performers, a couple of guys who really understood and got the power of positivity. One was an estate agent, and the other was a financial adviser. They were sitting there with positive attitudes and positive body language, engaged and ready to interact. In the middle of them, the less energised delegate sat with his head bowed, arms crossed and defensive. The other two listened intently and made notes, he didn't.

I was teaching some brilliant concepts and my two go-getters were writing them down, enthusing about them and talking about how they could use them in their respective businesses. Every few minutes the guy between them was putting his hand up and explaining why the strategies would not work for his business. He was totally negative.

But I noticed that every time he came up with a negative comment and a reason why he couldn't do something, the other two would look at him almost in disbelief at his attitude. Normally, I'd call someone like that out and address their negative attitude but in this case, I didn't because I could see what was going to happen. I knew the environment around him was so good that he'd have to rise to it. Soon, every time he gave a reason why something wouldn't work, the other two gave him a reason why it would. Over time, his body language started to change. His arms unfolded. He started to take notes. He rose to the environment. He realised that in the environment he was in, his negativity was not tolerated. He changed his behaviour and his attitude changed. The environment reprogrammed him. He knew he was with winners.

So how do you know who to surround yourself with and who to take advice from? Sometimes people who may appear difficult can offer excellent advice and have a positive impact, even though at the time you don't think they do.

My personal rule is that I don't take advice from anyone if I wouldn't want to swap places with them in the situation I am asking for advice about. For example, if I wanted advice on cooking, then I'd look for someone who is not only a better cook than me, but someone I'd want to be if I was a cook. If it was advice about relationships, I'd want to get advice from someone in the kind of relationship I'd hope to be in. If I wanted advice on how to make money, I'd look for someone who has made more money than me. If I wanted advice about fitness, I'd want somebody who is stronger, faster and fitter than me.

And when you do seek knowledge transference from others, it's not just about a quick chat or an email. Sharing knowledge works best when you share experience.

I illustrate this with an exercise I do in the social media branding events I deliver. I ask the room if there is a good baker present. Inevitably a few people will put their hands up. "So, if you were to cook something, you've probably got a signature dish?" I'll ask. Someone will answer. Maybe they'll say they can bake an amazing carrot cake.

"I'm not a good baker, but I want to make this amazing carrot cake," I'll say, "there's obviously a process isn't there? Can you explain what it is? Would you be able to show me?"

And they will tell me that I need ingredients and that they must be in the right amount and used in the correct order.

"What if I don't have the right amounts?" I'll ask.

"It won't work," is the likely reply.

"What if I get things out of sequence?"

"It will go wrong," they reply.

They take me through the ingredients and the sequence, and I will ask the right questions to illustrate just how much of a mess I could make of the process if the instructions are not absolutely clear. Then I'll ask if they think giving me the recipe and letting me follow it would result in a carrot cake as amazing as the ones they cook. By that point, the jury is usually out on my ability to follow a recipe successfully.

"Would it be better, then, if I came into the kitchen? If I stood next to you and you made the carrot cake with me? If you took me through the process?" I will then ask before I explain that is what the workshop will be like. That we'll be working together.

The exercise illustrates that even though you need the information and the ingredients and the sequence, you need the person too. If you find the right person who can give you the solution, and if you include them in your environment so you can learn from them, life becomes much easier because you get a transference of knowledge.

That's why, through my journey to success, I've had mentors and paid coaches who have influenced me and taught me different things. I have made it a habit to frequently seek out people who are operating at a higher level than me and spend time with them, building relationships and making friends with high level people.

One important skill for success associated with this is the ability to be coachable. This is something I learned and is a common trait in successful people. If there is someone who has a certain skill set that I respect and want to acquire, I will seek them out, ask questions, show respect, and take notes furiously to learn from them. Many people do not take that approach. Instead they look for ways to belittle, they may say things like 'they were lucky', or 'they are only succeeding because…'.

Successful people understand that those with skills they require are a resource. Choose the people in your environment wisely and they will help you grow.

MILLIONAIRE
SUCCESS SECRETS

- Everything you want in life will come from other people, don't be an island.
- Choose your inner circle wisely - Surround yourself with 5 positive individuals, and you'll become the 6th, Spend time with 5 negative people, and you will also become the 6th.
- Surround yourself with successful individuals; your path to success is paved by the company you keep.
- Seek out experts in what it is you need to succeed; they can give you the transference of knowledge you need to boost your success.

6

The quest for Knowledge – Ideas, Mindset and Information

I left school without qualifications and with no direction, but by the age of nineteen I had developed a thirst for knowledge that became unquenchable. The more I learned when I was being trained at Ford, the more I realised that information was one of the vital keys to success. If you had the right information and applied it in the right way, you could create a clear path to achieving goals. I can't pinpoint the exact moment I had my information lightbulb moment, and it was more likely a progressive realisation, rather than an epiphany. However, the training that the man from MarTech provided made me realise how empowering knowledge can be when applied in the right way. He was meticulous in the way he sat with me, identified the weaknesses in my technique and gave me the tools to correct myself.

I became hungry for knowledge and started reading as many books as I could get my hands on to learn new techniques and gain new insights. Success is a psychological process, as is sales. In order to achieve both, I realised I needed to understand some of the underlying psychological processes at play in the human mind. I went out and started buying sales books in a quest for guidance.

One of the first guides that made an impression on me was *Selling to Win* by Richard Denning. It is widely accepted as one of the classic and most influential books about sales and marketing ever written and I'd recommend it to anyone starting out on a sales or marketing career. It was first published in 1988 and has been revised and updated regularly. According to the author, there are six cylinders of a professional salesperson. These are business knowledge, industry knowledge, company knowledge, product knowledge, selling knowledge and attitude. I used the book as my gospel, and I started to put every bit of advice it gave into everyday practice. And it worked. My performance improved. It was a revelation.

I started to expand my library, reading more sales books. I read Tom Hopkins. His book, *How to Master the Art of Selling* has been a success bible for hundreds of thousands of people since it was first published in 1979. In the book, the author explains that after failing during the first six months of his career in sales, he discovered and applied sales techniques that earned him more than one million dollars in just three years. His book sets down the key secrets of his success, which include the need to escape from a fear of failure. It helped me understand how selling can become not just a job but a way of life that leads to greater success, greater satisfaction, and greater happiness.

By applying the information I gained from these books, I started to build skills that the other people in my working environment just didn't have. I started to master sales as I got to know more about its underlying elements. I started listening to training CDs and tapes. I was on a quest to expand my mind and I started to look for tips and patterns in the lives of successful people that would help me become more successful in my life. I started to read the autobiographies of successful people whom I admired and wanted to be like. I read Alan Sugar's autobiography, which impressed me so much it influenced my decision to apply to work with him.

By the age of twenty-one, filled with all this ambition and knowledge, I felt I'd succeeded in my job at Ford and was frustrated that I couldn't go any further. I was hungry. I wanted to do more.

Could I learn how to sell? Yes, I could, and I did. Could I learn how to build relationships? Yes, I could, and I did. Could I learn how to train people? Yes, I could, and I did. If there was something I didn't know, I found out the information.

It felt like I had found the key that unlocked a secret world of knowledge. I went from somebody who could never apply myself to learn at school to a true student of books. All it took was the right motivation. At school, I wasn't interested in the subjects they taught because I couldn't see how they were relevant to my life.

Now, I was reading like a maniac, absorbing everything I could get my hands on. I always had my head in a book and was always studying to improve myself because now I could link it to something that mattered to me, which was earning money and being successful.

The acquisition of knowledge became a theme that ran through my professional life in subsequent jobs and business ventures. Today, in my role as a wealth coach, international speaker and inspirational business leader, I share what I've learned with the people I mentor and coach. Back then I started attending courses. Now I run my own. I've created a virtuous circle of knowledge.

I sought knowledge from the best, which is why, at my own considerable cost, I started attending courses run by Anthony Robbins, a megastar of the motivational speaking circuit.

I invested in this type of training for my own self-improvement while I was working for other people. This is something I would recommend everyone does. Often, I will meet people at my events who want more from life and want to go on to achieve success and want to join my programme. They say that they will ask their employer to pay to put them through my programme. 99% of the time these people will not get to develop themselves further because they give control of their future to the company they work for. They are allowing someone else to decide if they can self-improve or not.

Success comes from this mentality - if it is meant to be, it is up to me. There is only one of you and as far as we know we only get one shot at life, so start developing you. Be your own greatest asset.

When I started attending some of Anthony Robbins' events, people tried to put me off. I was told they were American hype. I was told it would do nothing for me. Others said I was joining a cult. Some thought I was stupid, and others just couldn't understand why I would want to go and spend five days in a room with 3,000 people working on myself.

I found that the naysayers had two things in common. They were typically not happy in their lives and relatively unsuccessful. And they had never been to any of these types of training, so they had no clue what it was all about.

This is not to say that I wasn't put off a little by the criticism. Sometimes other people's opinions can make you doubt yourself and your decisions, so you have to create your own reality and trust your own instincts. Alternatively, when asking for advice, look at the person advising and say would I love to be where they are right now and if the answer is no, ask someone else whose shoes you would like to be in.

Back to Anthony. His techniques delve deep into psychological processes such as neurolinguistic programming and his courses incorporate firewalking, in which delegates walk over hot coals. He is the king of positive mindset, and his courses were the catalyst for me to start looking at my life and the direction I was heading and eventually deciding that I wanted to start my own business. More than anyone else, Anthony Robbins helped me learn about my abilities and made me confident that I could do anything I wanted if I learned how to do it and applied myself to the task.

I came back from his courses full of enthusiasm and ideas.

He talked about the power of the mind and being able to control it. He was the teacher who first made me aware of correct question techniques. Looking back now, much of it is common sense and simple stuff, the problem however is that common sense isn't that common. And back then, to someone who had never been exposed to ideas about psychology, it was mind-expanding. I found it very powerful.

I started to adopt the ideas in everyday life. You should too. For example, are you asking yourself the right questions? What story do you tell yourself about why you can't do something or why you can't succeed? When presented with a task do you say: 'I could do that, but I haven't got the time'? That is a common story people will tell themselves. But what happens if you ask a different question? What happens if you ask: 'I want to do this, how can I find the time'? The issue is reframed, and you will come up with a way of finding the time.

This small technique allowed me the ability to start controlling myself, and my reactions to things that happened in my life. It allowed me to do more and be more successful. I'd encourage people to do the same and to gain an understanding of how to ask better questions.

I developed an understanding of human psychology and picked up rules and maxims. One that stuck was, 'you don't get your shoulds, but you do get your musts'. What does it mean? Well, if you say to yourself: 'I *should* do this', you won't. If you say to yourself: 'I *must* do this', you will.

Robbins also took delegates through something called 'personal power'. This was a method that encouraged self-control and the belief that we can all do whatever we want, whether that's the power to go on a diet and actually see it through, or to quit smoking and actually see it through. He even taught that everyone has the power to make money and see it through. It's about creating the disciplines that allow you to get what you want from life.

As I've progressed on my success journey, I've spoken to lots of other successful people and in the early days of preparing for success Anthony Robbins stuff works. I am certainly appreciative of the lessons I learned early on, although for me to progress further, I found that I needed more strategy.

My takeaways from Anthony Robbins and other professional motivators were self-control, self-belief, and confidence, which are all qualities that can carry you to places in life but are ultimately limited, so my search continued in many other places.

My learning journey also helped to instil me with more confidence because after my experiences at school, I had assumed I just wasn't cut out to learn. It helped me understand that some people are slower learners than others and that different people learn in different ways.

My son is a good example of this. He learns in a different way but can still learn if the right techniques are applied. For Sammy it's all about security and having the correct structure. When he was first diagnosed with autism it was a huge shock for me, largely because I didn't understand his condition. Why has it happened? What does it mean? When you don't have the right information, you can be prone to fill in the blanks with assumptions. Sammy's mum was really good and started learning about his condition and what we needed to do to make his life normal. We haven't been together since Sammy was five. He's eight as I write this and that meant that I spent a lot of time with him on his own. In order to make him as happy and secure as possible, I started to learn about autism and when I did, it was no longer scary. Now it's not an issue at all; he's a very happy little boy and we have a wonderful, close relationship. I try to reinforce in him that he can achieve whatever he wants, he can be whatever he wants, and he can do whatever he wants. I encourage him and I try to give him positivity and self-belief.

I got great advice on parenthood from Gemma Collins' mum, Joan. We were having a chat one day and Joan had seen some of my posts on social media in which I'd been talking about my boy.

She's raised two successful children, Gemma, and her brother Russell.

She said to me: "I told my kids continually that they could be whatever they wanted in life and could achieve whatever they set their hearts on if they worked hard to achieve it. And I've raised two of the most confident people I know with loads of self-belief."

So that's what I try to do for Sammy because I want him to believe in himself and be happy. If he's successful, good. If he isn't, that's fine, as long as he's happy. There's no pressure for him to do anything he doesn't want to do.

The point to all this is that you must figure out the best method for learning for the individual you are. Once you know what works, there are no limits.

The other thing that I started to understand about myself as I started to study psychological processes was that I am an incessant questioner. When I was a kid people would always tell me to stop asking so many questions.

"Adam. You're driving me mental with all your questions!" was a common refrain.

I wanted to know everything. Why did you do that? Why did this happen? What's that? What does this do? I always wanted people to explain why they were doing certain things. I assumed that it was because I was generally an irritation, but I know now that it was because I am a very inquisitive person. And that's a good thing to be. If you accept things at face value, you don't learn. If you ask the questions to drill down and get the information, you learn. If no one ever thought to question why and how birds can fly, we'd never be able to get on a jet and go around the world!

Asking questions was my way of learning, of processing and of figuring things out.

One of the most important things you can do if you want to be successful in a certain field or endeavour is to feed your mind. Because contrary to the saying, it does not go in one ear and come out the other. It goes in, it rattles around, it sticks, and it dictates your choices. So, be careful about what goes in. Think of your brain as the engine that drives you and your body. Put in the right fuel and it will run efficiently. The more that you feed your mind with positivity, books, information, podcasts, whatever it might be, the more informed you will be and the better choices you'll make, which creates more chances for success.

I discovered all this as I learned more about my passion, which was sales and success. I became consumed by the subject. I would be at a party, and all I was thinking about was making money and success. I'd be out with my girlfriend. All I was thinking about was money and success. To be honest, it wasn't great for relationships. I became incredibly driven, and probably not great company. I was not thinking about the girl I was with, or about having fun. For a long time nothing else mattered to me. I was happy like that. I felt like I knew something that other people didn't know. I felt like I didn't want to be average anymore.

The more I learned, the more I started to realise that there were definite strategies to success. In sales and business, these strategies centre around the key themes I've already mentioned - specialised information(learning), environment (people and place), taking action and persistence. The mistake lots of people make is that they think they have to have a killer idea in order to succeed and they expend all their time and energy trying to find that one big idea. The truth is that you don't have to invent something new, novel or revolutionary, or provide a service that no one else provides in order to make a successful venture. In fact, it is best not to. Why gamble with something unproven when you can do something that you know works?

The idea is one percent of the success journey. That's all. And that comes as a surprise to many people. But at the end of the day, an idea is just an idea. It sits in your head and achieves nothing. The real skill is turning that idea into something tangible. Anyone can have an idea. Not everyone can turn that idea into success. Having an idea that sits in your head gets you nowhere. Ninety-nine percent of the things you do after that idea will dictate whether it works or not. This is why the idea really doesn't matter.

If you want to start a business that's successful, stop worrying about having a unique proposition because all you need to do is find a problem and provide a solution to that problem. Do that effectively and people will buy your solution. The quality of the solution and the experience you provide the customer are the things you can do to ensure success.

Back when I first started thinking about establishing my own business, I would torture myself trying to work out what the million-pound idea was. What could I do that no one else had done? I convinced myself, as have millions of others, that there are certain ideas that are rare and precious gateways to riches, like golden eggs. You find one of these ideas and success is guaranteed. But that's not how it works. The best way to create a successful venture is to either provide a solution to a problem or improve something that's already there in some way. My advice to the people I coach is look at different business models that make money and find out how they make money and what can be done to improve them. What can you do differently? How can you add more value or alternatively, how can you market it better? Because if there's a need there's a market.

To give an example, I had a Gold Circle client who was an immigration officer and helped people with their immigration and visa applications. He had been doing the job for thirteen years and was running his own consultancy. He did a lot of pro bono work and he wanted to expand and start monetising his business more effectively. The first stage I took him through was research. I asked him who his clients were, and he explained they were a broad base of people from lots of different backgrounds who had many different needs. We looked at those needs and there were countless different areas of immigration that his customers wanted help with. From there we identified which of the services he provided was the most profitable and which inquiries for which visas would lead to the best deals. Once we'd identified this, the next stage was to establish if there was a demand. We knew this to be the case because my client had serviced many customers. To be doubly sure, I checked using an online 'Answer-my-question' tool which confirmed that thousands of people had Googled questions about this specific type of visa but that no one had answered those questions. Instead, the answer lay in scores of pages of government policy. That proved that there was a definite demand for that type of service. I then went online to see what other businesses were advertising similar services. There was nothing. So, we had established that this was an area where there was a need, a profit and a demand that was not marketed. It was a niche that had no marketplace, which meant it was wide open to be marketed. All I had to do to get that guy's business up and running was to spend some money on Google ads and get his website optimised to address the problem. He went from running a business that had been treading water for thirteen years and kept going by word of mouth to explosive growth. And it didn't need an original idea.

If you can market it better or add more value, people come to you because they're getting more for their money. But it's got to be value to them, not value to you. To illustrate this, another of my Gold Circle clients runs a marketing company. Marketing companies are two a penny, so he needed to stand out from the rest. In order to do this, we positioned him as the UK's only risk-free marketing company. We told clients that if we market their business and they are not successful, we will give them all their money back. We did this because we looked at the marketing services available and investigated the main reasons why potential customers chose not to engage them. The main reason was that potential customers were worried they would not get a return on their investment. By offering a risk-free service, we encouraged the clients to take the plunge and engage, even though my client was more expensive than the others. That didn't matter so much when people realised that if it didn't work, they would get their money back. We agreed on the KPIs, that the customer's website would receive more traffic which we could show with Google Analytics. If traffic didn't grow, the client didn't get charged. The strategy added value for the customer, not the business, and did not involve a revolutionary idea, just some clever marketing.

Finally, in this section about ideas, mindset and information, I want to address ego, because another lesson I learned was that it doesn't matter how good you are or how good you think you are, you must learn to control your ego in order to make better, more objective decisions. When you start attaining success in any aspect of life, it's easy to fall into the ego trap and to believe your own hype. There is a fine line between being self-confident and self-assured and being egotistical. As best as you can, when you devise strategies and make decisions, try to take yourself, your wants, needs, and opinions out of the equation. Use hype to market things by all means, but don't believe the hype when the hype is about you!

This is best piece of advice I received when I interviewed Randy Zuckerberg, the former Director of Market Development and spokesperson for Facebook.

MILLIONAIRE
SUCCESS SECRETS

- Embrace Lifelong Learning – Go all in to master new skills.
- Cultivate a desire to learn what you need to know to achieve success.
- Seek out the right information.
- Use spare time to mind feed. When you are in the car, listen to a podcast. When you are in the gym, listen to an audio book.
- Replace 'should' with 'must,' and ask the right questions. Your self-talk is as vital as your outward communication.
- Ideas are one percent of success; everyone has thoughts but it's acting on the thoughts that make you successful.

7

Training Ground

After my brief interlude in the world of private jet leasing, I came back down to earth in an industry I was familiar with: car sales. I was twenty-two, I had shined at Ford, and I went to work in the BMW showroom in a place called Sytner Harrod Wood, in Essex on the outskirts of London. The showroom serviced some of the more affluent parts of the county, including Brentwood, where much of *TOWIE* was set. It had plenty of wealthy customers.

After excelling at the job at Ford, I assumed the job at BMW would be easy, with more of the same. I had a toolkit of skills that I'd gleaned from the sales books I had read and was looking forward to showing my new colleagues what an asset I would be.

The showroom, and BMW in general, was a success breeding ground. Many people I worked with there went on to achieve huge success. For example, the environment produced Gemma Collins who went from receptionist to TV star and entrepreneur. And another salesman I worked with there now lives around the corner from me in his own 14,000 sqft mansion. Countless other former colleagues started their own companies and became very successful, which is testament to the management and the way the company was structured.

BMW taught me advanced and effective sales techniques which were completely different from the methods used at the

Ford franchise. Everybody was treated well, and with respect. New staff were encouraged and nurtured. Everyone was valued.

My first impression when I walked into this environment was one of disbelief. I could not believe what I took to be a lack of work ethic. I had been drilled, military-style, to put in the hours and work very hard.

At the Ford job you stayed until you'd made all your calls and done all your admin. 13-hour days were not unusual. Often, I'd be in the office at ten at night on the phone because I'd been told that the more conversations you have, the more sales you make. I came out of Ford like a machine with strategies and tactics for increasing sales. Then I went into a new environment at BMW, and everything seemed sort of relaxed. After my brief interlude at AMSAIR, I was hungrier than ever and wanted to take this new world by storm. In my mind I was rubbing my hands thinking: *I'm going to smash this.*

There were four managers at BMW. Ivan, Chris, Lisa and Mark. Chris had been the number-one salesman for years and earned hundreds of thousands of pounds a year. And he was good, but I didn't rate him that much, which I would later discover was a huge mistake. Chris had been promoted and was now part of the management team.

When I first met him I just couldn't figure out the hype, but everyone else seemed to be convinced he was something special. He was a loud jovial type of person who seemed very forthcoming in introducing himself to everyone. He wore jet-black suits and always looked immaculate. He had a closely shaved head and wore a bi-metal gold Rolex Submariner watch. Despite being friendly, he seemed to move in and out of intense focus and I never quite knew what I would get when I spoke to him.

With Chris having moved up to a management role, there was a new top salesman on the showroom floor, a guy called James (he's the one that now lives in the big house around the corner I mentioned). James and Chris were close friends. Gemma was the receptionist and there was another receptionist called Jo.

In my egotistical arrogance, I looked around and thought I was better and more driven than any of them because their approach to the business seemed very slow. They would spend countless hours with clients and the rest of the time everyone seemed like they just didn't work that hard.

I was counting the riches I'd make before I even started. And the opportunities were immense. If I sold a BMW, the commission was £300, ten times the amount I earned at Ford.

On the first day at work, they gave me a 7 Series 750i long wheelbase to take home. It was a £100,000 car.

"Drive this one tonight because you've got to learn the product," I was told. "And the best salesman gets the best car, whatever model you want."

I was buzzing. I was so confident it seemed like a done deal. I was going to be king of the showroom.

It soon became apparent that my confidence was misplaced. What I failed to understand is that selling Ford Fiestas and selling high-end performance cars were two very different propositions.

Nevertheless, I attacked this new role in the way I had been taught. I worked very hard, made endless calls and was first up to see every customer. I spent zero time talking or building relationships with other team members and focused solely on bringing in the numbers. I worked late every night making calls and deals and outworked everyone. As a consequence I started well but despite my focus, discipline and work ethic, I just couldn't get to number one.

There were 12 other salespeople in the business and James was always top. In the first few months I hovered around number three or four. I did well but the competitive streak in me wanted the number one spot. Each month it evaded me. It was frustrating. I didn't understand why James and a couple of the others were beating me.

James seemed to swan in and out of the showroom. He was always laughing and joking around with the team and customers, and I just couldn't figure it out. He had Chris and some of the other management team as allies, but I didn't want that to be an excuse. It just seemed that no matter what I did or how much I sold, every time I did a deal James seemed to pull two or three more out of nowhere.

One of my weak spots at Ford had been building relationships with the customer. But in that environment it didn't matter so much. The managers there had rectified it to a degree by refusing to give me a price on part-exchange cars until I'd found out some extraneous details about the customer.

At BMW in one of my reviews with the management, it was picked up again and I was urged to talk to Chris, which I did. Rather than bawling me out for inadequacies, he started coaching me. It was a very different experience. It was like being mentored. Under Chris' tutelage, I began to realise that the BMW method of customer interaction was completely different to anything I'd seen before in every way, shape and form. It wasn't a structured, staged process. It was looser and more informal. There was a system for building relationships, selling and then keeping clients. It seemed so alien to me at first. I just did not believe that the system worked. I came from a different sales world, and I had to adapt.

Initially, I struggled. I thought I'd win by a mile, but I was completely wrong. I was doing it the wrong way. I had to have coaching to understand that my methods would not take me to the top in this new environment, and it took me longer to get up to speed because my beliefs about successful selling were completely different from their beliefs.

"Adam," they said, "it's long sell, short close."

I knew every closing technique there was. I had studied them and put them into action but none of that mattered because the point of the service at BMW was that we did not close customer sales. They closed themselves. The art of the BMW sell was to build such a great relationship with the customer that they wouldn't dream of buying somewhere else.

I applied myself and, within a short space of time, I had become number two in the company. James was number one still and it drove me mad. Even when I thought I was getting it right, I was still not where I wanted to be.

I had a heart-to-heart with Chris and asked him what I was doing wrong.

"You're still not there with the relationship building," he said.

"But I'm trying. I try to build a rapport," I explained.

"You've got to focus on the relationships. You have to build them. Look Adam, this is the thing, you don't care about the people."

"I do," I retorted.

"Be honest. You don't *really* care," he said. "You still care more about the money. That's where your heart is really at. You care about the money, and you care about being number one, but you do not really care about the people, and you will not be number one until you actually care about the people. When you care about them properly, I promise, you'll be number one. But until you fight for them, you'll always stay at number two."

I did some reflecting and I had to accept that my primary motivations were exactly as he said, money and being the best. What he was trying to explain is that all the time those were my focus, I couldn't truly focus on the customer and provide the type of service that people expected from BMW, because ultimately, I wanted the sale.

Once I understood that, I started to really concentrate on the customer. I started to care about the people and what they wanted. What I started to realise was that this relationship-building technique really worked. Because the relationship became reciprocal. When a customer knew I cared about them, they wanted to do more business with me. They wanted to refer their friends and colleagues to me. They wanted to get their other vehicles from me.

It was a shift in my perspective and an understanding of how relationships based on sales can work and it changed everything for me, even beyond my working life because although this is a story about my work, it also provides an important lesson in life. You have the power to set your own pathway to success by the way you treat the people around you. The most successful relationships are the relationships that you build with empathy and understanding and with mutual goals in mind.

Chris had helped me in many ways and his input allowed me to see things differently.

When I understood this, I excelled at BMW. There was always a tussle between James and me for the number-one spot and in the years that I worked at the company the sales pendulum swung between us. In my final year at BMW James and I slugged it out and I am pleased to say I came out on top.

In March one year, I did so well I made over £16,519 in one month. The management team asked if I minded this being shared and I said no problem. They held an entire team meeting and held up my pay slip. At 24 I had a choice of whatever new car I wanted. I was earning great money and finally building good relationships with the people that worked there. Chris and I became great friends. Brad from Ford came over to join us and I loved working with him again.

They were great days. I learned so much. My life changed further. Since Powerhouse, it had been on a trajectory that only ever went up. After I'd been there for around two years, I was asked to train Gemma, who was moving over from reception to sales. The bosses had seen untapped potential in her as they had in me. We worked closely together and while I taught her about the importance of relationship building – because like me she was initially focused on the money – she helped me with lifestyle advice.

Thanks to Gemma, I started to develop a taste for the finer things in life, which earning over £100,000 per year allowed me to buy.

I liked designer clothes. To this day I'm one of the few blokes I know who does genuinely enjoy shopping! I bought watches; I moved into a lovely flat; I ate in gourmet restaurants and went to some beautiful places on holiday. I loved traveling and seeing new places because I'd never had holidays growing up. When we were living in that café, my mum would go to America and leave the three of us kids behind. She went to Mauritius and left us behind too. I can't say I blame her; we were tearaways, and she deserved the break.

I didn't think that my life at the time was particularly extravagant. I knew I had a good standard of living and I deserved it, because I worked hard. I cultivated the attitude that if I was going to buy something, rather than say: 'what should I have?', I asked: 'what is the very best?'. If it was a watch, I wanted the best watch. I didn't want average, or medium. I wanted the best.

My aspirations were expanding, and my mind was expanding too. I was in a different place to my peers. The dream I'd had many years previously, of having an office job, had long since been achieved and I was on a journey as my goals, ambitions and dreams changed and grew.

I started to believe that I was special and that I was unique. I thought that I was invincible. My ego was in control, and I thought I could do anything I wanted.

Around the same time, I had started to attend the Anthony Robbins courses, which empowered me further with the belief that I was indestructible and would succeed no matter what. I started to develop a mindset that told me I couldn't fail. I was King Midas. Everything I touched would inevitably turn to gold.

I think that this egotistical view I had of myself may have developed when I was younger when I hung around with friends who got into trouble and got arrested, and I never did. They would say to me, "Adam, you are untouchable. You always get away with it. You're lucky." That was how I felt in life. I was blessed. It took constant achievement at work to bring this out in me.

And after three years of success at BMW, being a star performer, I started to think about the next step. Many of the wealthy clients I spoke to ran their own businesses, and that seemed like the next natural move for me. I had no doubt that if I did start my own business I would crush it in the same way I had at Ford and at BMW. I didn't know what I was going to do, but I knew that whatever it was I could not fail to be successful. There was no question, I was successful at everything. It was arrogant, but that was the mentality I had at the time.

It became all I could think about. Once, I was on a stag-do with mates in Newcastle-upon-Tyne walking through the town and I saw a sign. It was pink neon with the word 'BIG' written on it in glowing letters. *I want my business to have a sign like that,* I thought. The word 'big' seemed to sum up everything I wanted to be. I was utterly consumed by wanting more. All I thought about was making money and being successful.

As I was plotting my next move, Chris left BMW and went to start his own training business. Another colleague, Craig, who worked in the corporate side of the business, left and started a financial services company that sold products and services for bigger companies. Basically, he was a financial adviser and a middleman. He made good money and the opportunities in that industry at that time meant there was potential to make a killing. I had excellent contacts built from several years of high-end relationship building with the wealthy Essex clientele set so it seemed like a no-brainer. Not only can I do it, I thought to myself, but I can do it *better.*

I did what most people do and I gave myself one more year to earn enough money so I could start out on my own with a decent pot to invest.

It was and I remember sitting there on the run up to Christmas, working out how I could earn £150,000 the following year. I figured if I did this, after tax I could save and have at least £50,000 to start my business with.

I figured out every last detail of how I was going to reach my target. How many people I needed to speak to daily, how many leads I would need to convert, how many phone calls I would need to make per day, the number of connections I needed. I made a list of existing clients who I could encourage to switch cars. It was my master plan and I went away on the Christmas break confident that after one more year of intense effort I was going to be my own boss. I felt like my plan was fool proof.

In the New Year I went back to work and we had a team meeting in which each of us was handed a new pay plan for the year. My heart just sank into my stomach when I opened it. The pay plan capped everyone's' earnings at £100,000. I couldn't believe it. They wanted more performance, but they wanted to pay less money. I was in genuine shock. It seemed a far cry from them holding up my payslip telling everyone the potential to earn was unlimited.

I really didn't want to leave there and then, so I sat down with the management team, and explained my concerns. I told them my plan to break £150,000, showed them my spreadsheet and I expected them to understand.

There had been one change to the management team and it was he who delivered the killer blow.

He simply said: "Adam, we get it, however what you need to understand is as a business, we can easily get three salespeople in for £150,000, rather than one. Last year you earned more than the Head Of Business. Yes, you're good at what you do, but it doesn't make business sense to pay you that when we could replace you for less."

In that one conversation, I checked out. I felt like the three years I had been there and the philosophy I had bought into had been destroyed. In that meeting my decision was made. I was going.

However, I had a problem. I needed equity to start my business. I started to realise that while my lavish lifestyle had been fun, it had done me no favours. I had spent money I could have saved to fund my new venture.

Since the first house I bought on the advice of my manager at Ford when I was 19, I had moved again and there was £50,000 equity in the house I owned at that point. I dwelled on it and decided to sell the house to release funds. I figured once I started making decent money, I would be able to buy a better one anyway. I spoke to my mum and told her my plan. She agreed that for a nominal monthly rent I could move back in with her. At the age of 25 I was going home, the first time since moving out at 15. I figured I was going to be a millionaire in five years so it didn't matter.

Let's go and turn fifty grand into a million pounds, I thought. That was my mentality. Anthony Robbins said that if you believe you will be a millionaire, you will be. So, I believed it. I had been telling people for years. It was inevitable. It was my destiny.

And so, with £50,000 – every penny I had – I set up a financial services company called Big Financial. It was early 2008. What could possibly go wrong?

MILLIONAIRE
SUCCESS SECRETS

- Celebrate your successes.
- Always listen to and respect the advice of those with more knowledge and experience than you.
- Discover your customers' true desires; it's not always what you assume.
- Learn to love people even if it's not natural to you, we are always stronger together.
- Your current perspective creates recurring outcomes. How you change is how you succeed.
- Plan every move and detail but be prepared to move fast if things change.
- Success is intentional, not accidental. Stay coachable and learn from those who have already paved the way.

8

Control Your Own Future

Information is vital, and I didn't have the right information. That was on me. I take full responsibility.

You don't have to be an economic historian to realise that 2008 was probably not the best year to decide to go into financial services.

The warning signs of an epic financial crisis were blinking steadily throughout 2007 and 2008, initially from the USA. In mid-September 2008, catastrophe erupted when the investment bank, Lehman Brothers, collapsed, sending shockwaves through the entire global financial system and beyond.

I had no inkling of the trouble brewing across the Atlantic when I set up my business but even before the collapse of the banking system, I was struggling.

The idea of the business was to sell financial services to clients. My previous experience in the sector was helping to arrange car financing and leasing deals. I knew that side of finance, but I didn't know how to get clients.

I'd sold my house and moved back in with my mum. I had £50,000 and at the start I felt quite comfortable.

My days were very different. My commute was about ten steps from my bedroom to the spare bedroom next door where I'd set up my desk and computer. It didn't take long for my discipline to wane. I started getting up later and finishing earlier. Like lots of people until recently, I'd never worked from home, and I found the adjustment difficult. I'd always worked in a structured environment. I'd always had the discipline of having to be somewhere on time. That disciplined work ethic soon faded away right in front of my eyes. I just wasn't working as hard. I started to take longer lunch breaks. I started to walk from my mum's house into town where I had lunch, which got longer and longer. Some days I had two-hour lunch breaks. I started getting up later. Eight a.m. became ten a.m. I finished at four p.m. rather than six p.m. A full day became half a day. And the irony is, despite my desire to be a millionaire by the age of thirty, I quite enjoyed life on easy street and I started to feel quite chilled out.

But I wasn't getting any results and in the back of my mind, a little voice was telling me to get my arse in gear and make some changes.

I realise now that the reason for my relaxed attitude was that I had no skin in the game. When you've got no skin in the game, you tend not to work to your full capacity. When you pay, you pay attention.

My mum noticed what was going on and was probably getting fed up with having me around the house, so she introduced me to a guy who had an office to rent. I knew I needed a reason to get up and get a routine. I needed to be somewhere. I needed to have a place of work. So, I rented a tiny little office next to a burnt-out shed for £300 a month.

You see, business is like a baby, in that, in order for it to grow, you have to feed it. But unlike a baby, it doesn't eat food. What a business eats is cash. If you don't invest anything in your business, it won't grow. It's very simple. When you start investing in your business, you become invested in it. One of Mentors, Sarah

Willingham's Husband – Michael, said to me 'business is just investing over and over, it's investing to create returns'.

I decided at that point that I was going to make an investment in my business, and I fed it £300 a month. For that I got a tiny, run-down space and a toilet that didn't work. But I started turning up every day at nine a.m. The limited space also allowed me to employ someone.

My first employee was Boyd, a childhood friend. Boyd is a lovely man. But whereas I had a disciplined work mentality, he didn't. He hadn't had all the basic training I'd received. I employed him to help me sell services and contact customers and he had a good attitude. He was upbeat and he wanted to do well, he wanted to succeed. But I just couldn't get the right performance out of him.

I thought it was me. I thought I was a terrible manager (and I probably was). I'd never managed before. But he didn't have the skill sets the job needed and I didn't realise that. It was hard because he was a mate but that's not a good reason to employ someone. It didn't work out, Boyd worked for me for a little while and then went back to where he worked best the building industry.

Unfortunately, it was a mistake I made time and again, employing friends and family who didn't have skill sets that I needed for the job.

But I persisted and hired another friend, Alan. We were mates running a business that had no customers. My money started depleting at the same rate as my confidence. I have no qualms in telling you that at that point, I felt I had made a huge mistake. It seemed like I couldn't do anything right for the first six months and it was hell.

I lost count of the number of times I wanted to quit. It was almost daily. I felt lost, confused, and overwhelmed. My winner's mentality all but disappeared and it felt inevitable that I was going to fail miserably.

Becoming a millionaire slowly seemed like a ridiculous pipe dream. My confidence and self-belief disappeared.

It was a very different environment from what I'd been used to because the products were different, and while sales follow certain rules and processes no matter what you sell, in my previous jobs the companies I worked for provided all the marketing, advertising and administration functions. Leads were delivered on a plate. All the sales teams had to do was convert them.

In my new role as MD and business owner, I had no one around me to deal with the admin and, most importantly, no one supplying the customers. I had never managed employees. I knew nothing about the financials, the VAT, the payroll. I didn't understand networking. I knew nothing about building a business. All I knew was how to sell and how to build relationships. I felt massively out of my depth.

Today of course, I understand what I was doing wrong. Not only were my colleagues under-skilled, but so I was I. In order for me to go from that crappy office to the millionaire's mansion I live in today, I needed five areas of expertise. These were: business strategy, branding, marketing, sales and knowing the numbers.

If you want to make a million pounds in business, these are the five areas that you need to work on. When I started, I didn't have a strategy. I didn't have the branding and I didn't have the marketing, but I did have sales. And so did my colleagues. We were sales-heavy with none of the other required skills.

We did try marketing and we improved. But it was a scattergun approach. It was word of mouth. We used direct marketing and sent out letters. We got some responses, but not enough. I did some email marketing and bought data lists, in the days when you could before GDPR. I even did crazy stuff like putting postcard ads in Tesco.

The biggest problem for me was that I had no idea how to get my message out.

Now I know this is not uncommon, as I train thousands of business owners a year. But when you're in it, you can't always see it. One of the reasons I enjoy helping people now is because I remember the feeling of hopelessness. It was awful. I remember scrapping around for business, being in a race to the bottom on pricing and living in a world where you commit your heart and soul to a business but have no idea what you are doing wrong.

Often, when I see a business that has no clients, be it a struggling restaurant or a shop with no customers, it takes me back to this place very quickly and hits me hard because I know exactly how it feels and it really isn't nice. One of the reasons I do what I do is so people can avoid this type of failure.

Despite feeling lost and confused, I would not quit. My seed fund was evaporating but I was committed, and I knew I had to find a way, so I started reading books about copywriting, marketing and direct mail. I frequently went back to what I did when I was at Ford and rang people cold. I went out and had meetings with different people. I made some industry contacts and even met one of my good friends and clients to this day, Kamran Saleem, who eventually became one of my Gold Circle members.

Some methods worked and bought in a few clients, but there's a big difference between having a method that works to get you some clients and to having a method that consistently brings you clients. And that's what I didn't have.

I employed another one of my friends whom I'd worked with at Ford. A guy called Bradley. Things started to pick up because Bradley had a wider skill set. He also had a customer base from Ford and the same discipline and training background as me. He was good with customers. He was good at everything. And he made me realise that it wasn't necessarily that I was a bad manager, it was that I was bringing in the wrong people.

Bradley eventually went on start his own successful business. Big Financial just wasn't offering him the consistency he needed. Some months were good, some months were not, but by the time he left, we had started growing. Alan recommended that I employ his girlfriend, Zoe, to come in and do the bookkeeping because I was bad with numbers. She started working for me and very quickly became my right-hand person. She was multi-skilled. She was good at sales, relationships, bookkeeping and she had a level of commitment that was impressive. She believed in the company.

My swagger slowly started to reappear. I started to think business could work out for me, I felt I'd made a breakthrough.

And then came that financial crash.

People started queuing up outside branches of Northern Rock trying to pull their money out. An earthquake was coming, and the entire financial industry would suffer the aftershocks. As Lehman Brothers collapsed and Northern Rock went into public ownership, the financial sector went into spasm and all the partners that I'd developed relationships with to sell their products and loans pulled out of the market, leaving me with nothing to sell, no one to sell to and no income.

I watched in horror each month as my pot shrunk. I just didn't know what to do. I was so sure I was going win at business, but the reality was, I sucked. I was terrible. It was a disaster. It was a boot to my confidence, and I started to question whether I'd hit my limit. I thought many times about going back to BMW with my tail between my legs. If I did, I thought I'd spend the rest of my life there and I associated that with failure. All I'd ever be was a car salesman, which is a noble profession but not one I wanted to spend the rest of my days doing. I realised that I didn't want that to be my story.

But the financial sector was a difficult industry to break into, even without a global financial crash. I needed to come up with another way to make money, quickly.

At the same time, Chris, my ex-manager at BMW who had started his business a bit before me, was doing well. This became the second time his advice made a huge impact on me. We had become friends at that stage and one night we went out for dinner where I did something unsuccessful people do all the time and I didn't even realise I was doing it. I decided to project my fears on to Chris. I told him how bad the economy was. I told him about the financial crisis, why it was a terrible time to start a business, how he should be careful. I moaned non-stop, coming up with endless excuses for my failure, rather than taking personal responsibility. I blamed it all on the recession.

He listened, for a bit and when he'd heard enough he asked me a question.

"Adam, do you know what a recession is?"

"Well, sort of I have been reading all about it," I replied.

"So what is it Adam?" he pushed.

"Well, it's a financial crisis Chris and it's bad for business," I said.

"I understand that, but for the country to be in recession, we need two quarters of negative growth in the economy," he explained.

"Okay," I said, "what's your point?"

"My point is, I am not taking part in that!"

I was confused and thought he was delusional at first, until he explained in the past six months his company had been growing regardless of the overall state of the national economy.

He then asked me whether my business was growing or shrinking. I told him that every month we managed to sell marginally more than the previous month.

"Well, you're not taking part either then, are you," he said, before leaning over to me and telling me that "Winners create their own economies".

I remember that conversation to this day because it switched my mindset. Others would have fear-mongered with me, moaned and whined, but Chris showed me the mentality I had lost.

We talked more and he agreed that I needed a plan B. He also encouraged me to start attending some of the business networking events that he went to. He had made some great connections from these which led to business opportunities for his company.

I thought about what else I could do to make some money and shore up my losses. I knew about cars. I knew how to sell cars and how to make money from selling cars.

Chris knew this too and made a proposal. He was doing so well that he was in the market for an upgrade, but he didn't have the time or the inclination to sell his car and scour through the ads for a new one.

"I'm looking for a Bentley," he said. "Why don't you sell my car, take a cut and find me another one, which I'll buy off you and you take a margin?"

His business partner was also looking for a car. He wanted an Aston Martin.

I went out and found an Aston Martin and a Bentley and fulfilled the orders, making a decent profit in the process.

Chris also took me to networking events run by an organisation called The Business Lounge. The outfit was run by a lady called Patsy and by another guy called Perry, who has since sadly passed away. He was the founder of the company Insure and Go and when he sold it, he used some of the money to fund The Business Lounge. He wanted to create a business network for high-level people where they could learn from each other and develop relationships. The events were held in places like The Shard and The Gherkin in London. We went to beautiful restaurants and at the events guests talked about business and discussed related topics. We delivered presentations on these topics to each other. I had never presented to people before and I felt out of my depth. Chris thrived at these events. He made connections, created opportunities and developed relationships with people to do business with, but I struggled to find anyone who would do business with me.

"Why doesn't anyone do business with me?" I asked him on the way to an event. He was the type of person who seemed to instinctively understand people and could analyse business situations and come up with solutions.

"Because you pitch your business wrong, you don't explain it properly," he said.

And this is one of the things that now I teach my clients.

"You don't explain what you do clearly enough. You don't make it compelling enough for them to want to do business with you. You have to sell the business; you have to sell yourself."

And he was absolutely correct. One of my key strategies to success now is that there are four things you need to sell when you are trying sell anything (in the same way that there are four stages of success). You need to be able to sell your business. You need to be able to sell yourself. You need to sell your product and you need to sell your level of service.

Using my situation as it was then as an example, I was able to sell a product – cars – but I wasn't selling a business, a service or myself.

Chris mentored me and, after another failed networking event, set me a task.

He said: "This is how I want you to position your business. I want you to tell the people at the next event that you are an estate agent for cars. That is what is going to pique their interest. And then you're going explain to them that you can get them more money back for their car than if they went to any other dealership because you will put it up for sale for them and get them the retail value. But in addition to that, you'll find their next car for them at a lower value by searching the entire marketplace, because you know how to bargain, and you have contacts in the industry that you've built up over years."

It was a great idea, but to begin with I resisted.

"But I'm *not* an estate agent for cars," I said.

"It's what you did for me. You found me a car and sold my old one. Trust me, just do it. They'll go for it," he told me.

I took his advice and at the next event I did a presentation on my business idea, pitching it as an estate-agency-style service for cars. Everyone in the room exclaimed what a good idea it was and before I knew it, I'd picked up several new clients. I could see that there was potential in the idea.

Zoe got it too. She took to the message like a duck to water because she had worked in an estate agency previously. She reached out to all her old clients and started bringing in new business.

Around the same time, I started reading about the commercial potential of social media. This was in the late noughties, before TikTok and Instagram, in the days when social media was still a nascent technology. The main sites in the UK were Facebook, Myspace and Twitter and most people used them to look up old school friends and their childhood sweethearts. But in the US, innovative businesses understood that social media was a whole new communications ecosystem that could allow brands to reach out directly to their customers or potential customers.

Chris showed me how to refine my pitch, but I needed a way to get my message out there. I felt like the world's best kept secret. I had a good message, but no one knew who I was. I needed a marketing method that was consistent and that was scalable. This led to inconsistency and that led to me losing Bradley.

At around the same time, I saw an advertisement for an event. It was a big personal development and success conference being held in London. There was a roster of speakers talking about moneymaking schemes such as foreign exchange (or forex) and property. I went there to get some motivation and inspiration. The speakers at the event were also selling courses and workshops that delegates could pay to sign up to.

I didn't set out to sign up for anything as I didn't have much money. But then a speaker came on and started talking about social media. He had a product called *Get 10,000 Fans*. It was a £5,000 three-day course in the US. It promised to show delegates how to market their messages, products and service on Facebook and pick up 10,000 fans.

As I sat there listening, I genuinely felt like the presenter was talking directly to me. There were 2,000 people in the room, but it didn't feel like anybody else was there. What he was saying resonated so clearly with me and the position I was in.

I decided to buy the course. I didn't have the money, but I put it across two credit cards. When I told my mum about the course in America, she offered me the airfare. She didn't have lots of money and what she did have she'd worked very hard to get so it meant a lot to me that she was willing to help me and believed in me.

I booked my flight and a few months later found myself in America at the course with 100 other delegates. Some people thought it was a gamble given the cost. Even though the car business and the finance business together were starting to pick up customers from contacts I made through The Business Lounge, I was still only just managing to survive. I was keeping my head above water, and everyone thought I was going to fail. I had given up a £100,000-a-year job and a top of the range BMW to start a business that was hardly earning anything. Instead of a 7 Series, I was driving a second-hand banger. But I was determined, and the idea of a car business built online started to develop in my mind. I knew the answers lay in the information I could learn from that social media course because much of the advanced business literature I was reading indicated that the future lay in online-based interactions. I needed to act and get to the right environment: that course in the US.

I wasn't disappointed. What I learned blew my mind. The speaker got up and started talking about social media and the opportunities it provided.

"Social media allows you to have mass conversations. This is the future. Instead of talking to one person you can speak to 2,000 people, one hundred thousand, a million! We can show you how to get 10,000 fans and you'll make more money," he riffed.

I was mesmerised because all I'd ever learned from the very early days was that the more people you speak to about yourself, your business and your service, the more money you can make. And here was a way of speaking to millions. And the best part was, it was easy. In all the jobs I'd ever done, speaking to people was about time and grafting, speaking to one person after another after another. With social media you speak to everyone all at once.

I devoured the information, and I became obsessed. I took my previous obsession with sales and marketing and transferred it to social media.

I knew I had a service and a product that added value to the existing car sales process but what I didn't have was customers. I knew that when I got the customers I could look after them, care about them and get results for them. I was going to Business Lounge dinners and begging and grafting to get one or two new customers.

The realisation of what I could do on social media with the techniques that I learned in the US lit a fire within me that carried on burning for several years. It changed everything.

The course also provided delegates with access to a membership site where you could log in, watch tutorials, and do lessons and activities online. When I returned home, I obsessed over each module. Learning for me was about repetition. Rather than doing fifty different courses, I believe you are better off finding one course that fulfils your needs and doing it 50 times instead.

When I was reading sales books at Ford, rather than buy ten books and skimming over them, I bought one really good one and read it several times until the information went in.

So, I watched the social media content again and I did exactly what it told me to do. And because of that I started to build up a following on Facebook. I got 10,000 followers on my Facebook page, so I then had 10,000 new people to talk to.

The thing that I learned in that course that changed my life forever was that the fastest way to make money, bar none, is to turn advertising into profit. When you turn advertising into profit, you never look back.

I built my Facebook page. I positioned it properly. I used the copywriting skills the course taught. I paid £100 on Facebook marketing to target the right people and I prepared for my first ever online sale, a Nissan. It was a Sunday evening and I got over 200 enquiries for that one car, which I sold that night. For my £100 not only had I sold the car and made several hundred back in profit, I'd also generated hundreds of solid leads because I realised that everyone who replied was also a potential customer, who most likely had a car to sell and who was looking for a new vehicle. I stayed up till one a.m. to answer all the enquiries. It was insane. I asked what kind of cars people were looking for and what they had to sell, and I walked into the business the next day to meet Zoe with fifteen new customers and details of the makes and models that each one wanted. Zoe then spent the whole day on the phone finding stock to fulfil those orders.

Our message was: "Well, this car is gone. What car have you got? We can sell it for you and find you another."

It was like a precursor of We Buy Any Car.

It is worth pointing out that this was in the early days of Facebook marketing and that £100 today will not get the results it did back then when things went crazy. I thought to myself if I spend £100 to sell one car and get fifteen new customers, what happens if I spend £1000? I soon found out. I was getting so many customers I had to start taking on more staff and moved to bigger offices in Chelmsford. I'd cracked the marketing secret and the business was born. In the following six months, we did a million pounds in sales. My life was changing fast.

MILLIONAIRE
SUCCESS SECRETS

- You need skin in the game; when you pay, you pay attention.
- You need great people in your team. Don't settle for good, go for great.
- Establish a routine, especially if you're self-employed and working from home. Routine fosters discipline.
- Know your limits and employ people with the skills you don't have.
- The business skills to develop:
  1. Strategy
  2. Branding
  3. Marketing
  4. Sales
  5. Numbers
- Perfect your pitch, grasp your business's essence and its value, and firmly establish your why.
- Social media is one of the most powerful tools your business has, learn how to turn ads into profit.

9

Drive Sales

From the start, I could see that the potential for business growth was limitless if I had the resources. With such a huge marketplace I realised that I could quickly become one of the biggest car sales businesses in the UK. I needed people, stock and space and within a few months had managed to build to a level where I was turning over massive amounts of stock.

The message to market was that our business was not a regular dealership. We sold your car for you and then we got you the car you wanted. I had people from all over the country driving down to Essex to bring their cars to me, which we'd put up for sale for them. We'd also sell them the car they were looking for. It was all second hand.

I had to understand our place in the market. I accepted that we were never going to compete with a Ford or BMW garage. Instead, we needed to give our customers a unique incentive, which was don't part-exchange your car with a franchise and get less for it. Instead, we'll sell it for you at retail value which will get you 20% more. We took 7.5% of the sale, or £1,000 minimum, as our cut and we made money selling them a new car. We also used the car they were selling to get new customers, so each transaction led to three deals. We also started offering finance and made money through that. We were, essentially, a broker.

The idea resonated. People realised they were getting a much better deal through us and within a year, I grew the business to £2.9m. The next year we did £4.3m and things started getting harder.

One of the most difficult things I faced was that stock was coming in so fast it was hard to keep track. Some of the cars had problems and needed work, which then chipped away at the profit margins.

There was such a volume of work that I ended up working every day. I was so busy; I had so many enquiries to answer. I got into the office at eight in the morning and would be there until eleven at night.

I had cash-flow stresses and the stress of trying to pay people. I was doing everything, and I was stretched to the max. I was angry all the time, but I was so driven that I just kept pushing through, hanging on for the ride.

The root of the issue, and the biggest problem I had, was that organisationally we were a mess. Logbooks would go missing, handbooks would go missing, spare keys would go missing. We were writing out cheques left, right and centre to pay for replacements. If a car broke down after we sold it, we were blamed. It was inevitable we'd have problems because we expanded so rapidly. We went from selling 10 cars a month to 60 then 80 very quickly. We were in a constant state of expansion.

At £4.3m turnover, I needed a bigger office and moved into a 3,000 sqft building with 25 parking spaces.

At the stage we were selling 50 cars a month. I got the stock inflow handled and we became more organised. I paid more attention to the systems and processes, and I found that things got easier for a short time.

Chris saw my business go from strength to strength. At the same time his business, which was based on government funding, was not doing so well. He started making overtures about wanting to work with me. I was not sure. I realised by then that hiring friends was not always a good idea, but Chris was a skilled salesperson so I bought him into the business.

When he came to work for me, his sales genius was clear to see. Within a few months he was selling 50 cars a month alone, taking us to over 100 vehicles a month. He became a driving force to push us on. When you bring A-players into your organisation, they tend to drive up standards.

With a better sales team and a large social media presence, we started to be viewed as an up-and-coming business, we also had more cashflow and the ability to build the team. People from my past approached me and were interested in what we were doing. Locally we attracted press attention.

Brad, who I worked with at Ford, joined as a sales manager. To this day he is genuinely one of my favourite people, the kind of guy you love being around. Back when I was the youngest at Ford, he helped me, despite him thinking I was crazy for having those big goals and dreams. When he started to see that I might just achieve them, he was keen to be involved.

Some people left as we grew dramatically and that is normal when a business goes into expansion mode and changes rapidly. Zoe left as she preferred being part of something smaller. The team changed and we started to make the business more professional.

During the early years between being a £1 million company to getting to £4.3 million, dramatic changes were needed in order to run the business the right way. I had to make hard decisions and change from being everyone's friend to being the leader. This change often creates friction for entrepreneurs, and it was something I struggled with. I hated how it changed my relationships with people.

There were many people during this stage who did a good job for me along the way, but who seemed to turn on me. I started to develop a little bit of a victim mentality. I feel this is an important lesson to share because as you build a business and start to become successful, some people start to behave differently towards you. People I had been close to started to do things that appeared be aimed toward hurting me, which I felt I didn't deserve.

For example, I hired one of my best friends who then decided to take the same business model and a large cohort of my clients and set up his own business, costing me a lot of money in the process.

People I treated very well and paid handsomely attempted to take me to court for money they didn't deserve and were not due while finance companies I partnered with approached members of my team and offered them terms to set up rival businesses. Two young lads who I felt I mentored and treated very well stole my database and set up a rival business. People I trusted took profits from the business as personal payments, stealing tens of thousands in the process. A Range Rover was stolen in very dubious circumstances after the sales executive who brought the car in part exchange for £25,000 didn't take a spare key. The car was stolen from where it was fortuitously parked at the back of the showroom by a thief who I assume used the spare key. Despite reporting it to the police I never saw an outcome.

Other members of the sales team failed to examine clients' driving licenses when applying for finance, only to discover the people purchasing on finance were not who they said they were.

This ruse cost the business nearly £50,000 repaying finance on cars that disappeared.

One of the final straws for me was when Chris left and set up a business on a similar model with another friend who was a client. Chris was a very close friend, a mentor and someone I supported when he went through a personal crisis, so it was very difficult to take.

These occurrences are just a few of many and I include them not because I am whinging, but because they helped to shape me. At that point in my life, they really did mess with my head. I didn't know how to handle them and couldn't understand why they were happening to me. Why would anyone want to do that to me?

At that stage, one of my clients introduced to me another mentor who helped me through. She was called Sue, and she helped me to understand human behaviour in a way I had never appreciated before. She helped me get rid of any bitterness and taught me to accept what had happened and move on swiftly. She helped me eliminate the victim mentality.

I realised that the more I moaned and griped to people about how unfair it all was, the more negativity I attracted into my life. I was making the same mistake again and again, hiring people I wanted to share my success with, rather than hiring people I didn't have personal links to. The personal relationships meant I was ignoring the red flags and letting people take advantage of me. People were drawn to me and my business because they wanted to learn how it was done, but this left me a wide-open target. I shared far too much with everyone. I lacked the strategies to protect myself and frankly, through errors in judgement, I got what I deserved.

This was an important lesson and through my work with Sue, I identified the right type of people to work within my business. I became a lot more strategic in building my teams. I let personal feelings about business go and started to see it more as a game. In order to win the game, you have to make the right decisions. This crucial stage of business helped mould who I am today. I don't take things personally. I don't let emotions get the better of me. I am very careful and strategic in who I recruit, and I am much more diligent in seeking partnerships. I make decisions faster. For example, if something is not going to work out and I have seen the red flags, I cut out fast. I will be polite and compassionate when there are people involved, but I will not change my mind once a decision has been made.

This is a trait that successful people have and something I know from personal experience is difficult to cultivate. When I started, I was a people-pleaser. I wanted to make everyone happy. I wanted to be liked. I wanted to be popular with my teams. I wanted to be loved. But as a leader, not every decision will be popular. Hard conversations need to be had and you need to be prepared to have them. Before I got to grips with this, if you crossed me, you crossed me for life. Now, if you cross me, you're gone with no second chances, but I'll say hello if I see you in the street.

Through cultivating this new skill, my problems seemed to evaporate. I stopped sweating the small stuff and made better decisions. Business got easier, growth became more manageable, my teams, processes and systems became more professional. We made more money and I got to enjoy the next year or two in business with significantly less problems.

It was at that stage, with the pressure off, that I was able to think long term. I invested in properties and took care of my long-term future with pension investments. I started to enjoy my success. I remember this period as being my favourite time in the car business. We made great profits, we had a great team, my problem team members moved on and I felt we were starting to create success, growing the business to over £6 million pounds per year.

MILLIONAIRE
SUCCESS SECRETS

- Business is a game.
- Remember, business may feel personal, but it's not. Play to win and keep emotions aside.
- What you put out; you get back. Keep focusing on the negative and you will pull more negativity towards you, focus on the positive and you will attract more positivity.
- Make firm decisions and commit to them; once it's done, it's done.

10

Know Your Numbers

O ne of the things I love about business, is perhaps something most people would not expect or share with me. It is the continual challenges business presents. Having now trained thousands of businesspeople and being familiar with the majority of business models, it is very easy to see that the car industry is fraught with challenges. One of the main reasons I came out of that business in the longer term, was the continual requirement for large amounts of funding, which exposes the owner of the business in a big way. After a relatively smooth year as a new improved business owner, who was smarter, tougher and a better decision maker, a new challenge started to present itself the problem of cash flow started to arise. I was managing £6m a year and was a great marketer at that stage. I was a great salesperson too and I started becoming a better leader and was much more in control of the business, but cash started to get tight. I was twenty-eight and out of my depth. We had around £1m of other people's cars up for sale and although they were selling, they never sold fast enough. We always seemed to be waiting for money and it meant we couldn't buy any of the part-exchanges that people were bringing in. I had virtually no funds in the business apart from the profit we were making. I needed to raise money.

I knew about stock funding loans provided by companies that loan money to businesses to help them buy stock and I set up meetings with several of them. But the problem was, the funders didn't like our model because they'd never seen it before. Plus, it was generally felt that I was too young and inexperienced.

I realised I needed to find somebody to come and work for me who understood the numbers. I spoke to a recruitment company and said, "I need the best. I need somebody who knows how to get funding and wants to come on a journey." I was sent the CV of a man called Richard who looked perfect on paper. He had plenty of experience in raising funds. He had helped another car dealership grow from nothing to a £30-million turnover company and had worked for main dealerships his whole life. He was well respected. He wanted £60,000 a year, which was more than I had ever paid anyone. I arranged to interview him but on the day of the interview the recruitment consultant called and said: "He had a look at your company last night and is sorry but decided it's not for him."

"If he can be here in the next fifteen minutes, tell him I'll give him £75,000," I replied.

That must have focused his mind because he came in to meet me and said, "Well, you're a bold young man, aren't you?"

He sat down with me, and I sold him the dream. I explained everything about the company, how we operated, our challenges and what we needed.

"I'll come in; I'll get you the money. You don't have to pay me the £75,000, I'll take £60,000," he said. "But if I do what I say I'm going to do, you can give me a bonus up to 75. I've got the contacts, the connections and the experience to get the funding. But when I get you the funding it is on the condition that you don't take the money out of the company and go and buy a big house. That's one rule. The next rule is that you remember that I'm the person that got you the funding, so don't replace me with someone younger in the next five years."

It was fair, he was asking for loyalty and recognition and for me to respect the terms of the loans he believed he could secure. Richard became our finance director and within the first two weeks of starting, he approached multiple different companies and set up a funding pack that we could send to finance providers which included all our financials. He got together a balance sheet, he put in cash flow forecast projections and details of all the team. He put a business plan together and gave us a mission statement and values. He created a sixty-page document that outlined why someone should give us funding. With all the correct groundwork in place, he raised me £2 million pounds worth of funding in a very short space of time. That, I learned, was the difference experience makes.

Richard provided what I needed to get me to the next level and I want to share with you the steps that were taken to make this happen

Richard helped me with a crash course in number skills and this is something that I discovered later that all top businesspeople have.

I remember the first day Richard came to work with me. He walked in with his typically imposing fashion, full of a confidence rarely seen in accountants and finance directors. He was 6ft 4in and wore an immaculate black pin-striped suit, a white shirt and a bold red tie. He looked like he meant business.

As he moved towards my small office, which I had tidied up in anticipation for his arrival, I noticed he was carrying something in his hand. It was a ruler made of transparent red plastic.

"Good morning young man. I have a gift for you," he said as he placed the ruler on my desk. Thoughts of maths lessons sprung to mind.

"This ruler is going to be your best friend," he said.

Having always been the leader of the business, always having been in full control, my first thoughts were, I am paying him to do a job not to tell me what to do.

Then he sat down on one of my funky purple branded chairs purchased from a fashionable furniture store and proceeded to explain to me where I needed to change.

"Adam, you're a young man, you are bold, and I like your energy, I have no doubt you are a great salesperson but being a great salesperson and being a great businessperson are different skillsets entirely" he said.

Trying not to take offence, I decided there was a time to speak and a time to listen. This was a time to listen.

He continued: "A great businessperson knows their numbers and makes decisions based on the numbers. Feelings lie to us and cloud our judgement, but numbers never lie. I don't need to be here, but I choose to be because I want to ensure that I make a difference and I feel I can do that with you. I want you to trust me and allow me to teach you about the numbers, so you make your decisions based on them. In doing so you will become stronger and achieve more than you can even imagine." He was like one of those Jedi masters in Star Wars.

It was another epiphany and another turning point for me. That week we barely left my office and analysed every detail of my business with the ruler. **I learned lessons that I use to this day and later I turned these lessons into a core part of how I help**

business owners to achieve success in the Numbers Pillar, with the system I call Numbers into decisions.

This is how he explained it to me, and I want to detail it for you so you can start to adopt these very simple ideas too.

1. ROI Investing

Richard pointed to the purple chair and said every expense that goes out of the business should accomplish one of two things; it should make money (create income) or save money (save income). He asked if the purple chair made us money or saved us money. I tried to explain the branding purpose of the decision to buy the chair. He explained there was a time and place for branding investments but right then, when cash-flow was tight, was the wrong time.

I told him I thought we needed more salespeople. At the time we employed four salespeople. He explained that investing in sales makes money.

"There is room for 12 desks, and we are going to calculate the ROI per head of every salesperson so we can make the decision if we need more or not," he said.

After doing a simple calculation we worked out that on average each salesperson cost us £3,150 per month but returned £16,200 in profit. It was an easy decision.

One of the common errors people make in business is to fixate on what something is going to cost, rather than what it will make. We looked at every aspect of the business and analysed the numbers. My decisions became easier. I was less stressed and got more of the decisions right. Business got a lot easier.

As we delved deeper into the numbers, we started looking at administration staffs costs, which I had always assumed were extra expense. But we discovered we were losing thousands a month in goodwill payments for mistakes and ordering crazy amounts of spare keys and handbooks. People were cancelling orders because of time delays and poor preparation. By solving these problems with a £20,000 a year admin person, we worked out we could save nearly £80,000 in mistakes that damaged the brand.

"The brand is your reputation not the purple chair my boy," explained Richard. That one stung a little.

The key to all this is that it is not what it cost you, it is what it makes you or saves you.

2. Margin Testing

Before Richard, I had purchased stock based on what I felt would sell. I had never really looked at what margins we made or the speed we made them.

I had resorted to purchasing bigger vehicles in the hope of getting bigger profits to sort out the cash-flow problems, but when we looked at the speed in which these vehicles sold and the amount, they sold for it was clear I had made mistakes. I had no balance in my product range.

Richard explained we needed to balance the margins and the number of days we kept the stock. We were not going to make purchases that didn't have the correct margins any longer. We put in minimum margin figures and started turning down bad business.

I see this pattern with my new clients who chase business in the early days of their enterprises. This brings bad clients and sparks a race to the bottom on pricing. They haven't learned to say no which means they end up being busy fools with clients who only come to them because they offer the cheapest deal.

Once we established our minimum margins and stuck to them, cash-flow improved, stock balance improved, and the business was on more solid ground.

This lesson applies in service industries too. You must have a decent margin in your product or service in order to create wealth and success.

To help you understand, let's say we set up a business selling handbags. We buy them for £4 and sell them for £10, giving a £6 margin.

However, that's just a small part of the story because there are costs attached which could be significant. You have to get the handbag to you - delivery in. You also have to get the handbag out to the client - delivery out. You might have to run ads to sell the handbag in the first place, which are marketing fees. You can already see that the margin is being eroded. It could be that your margin becomes untenable if you have too many peripheral costs. That's not to say there is no money in handbags. If Chanel sells one for $5,000, there is plenty left over for the extra costs because they have a higher margin and are selling at a higher ticket price.

All my years in business have led me to the conclusion that it is much easier to build a profitable business selling items that carry higher margins or higher ticket prices.

Based on the handbag example, in order to do £1million in sales, your company has to sell 100,000 units at £10. Chanel only has to sell 200 units at £5000. Your company has cash-flow issues because the extra costs are cutting into the margin while Chanel has bundles of cash because of its high margins. In addition, it's easier to find 200 wealthy clients than 100,000 budget clients.

In summary, set appropriate margins and sell at a higher ticket price to attain your success faster.

3. Looking forward how to predict the future in business

Once we had set the margins we started looking forward and planning out what we wanted to achieve.

I wrote my first ever budget. This is now one of the first things I do with any business I run. I wouldn't dream of running a business without one.

Richard explained to me that most businesses run for the entire year and then wait for the accountant to tell them if they did well or not. This is a HUGE Mistake and one you should avoid, because if you wait a year to find out you are not doing okay, it is too late to rectify the situation. Instead, a business owner needs to look forward and make sure they track the performance at least monthly to see if the objectives are being met.

At this point you may be thinking, *Adam I haven't started my business yet.* Or *I'm too small to be putting these things in place*, or even, *my accountant does this for me.*

Don't fall into this trap. Adopt these principles now. I wish I had done so earlier in my career. As soon as I took these lessons on board and introduced them, they helped me to achieve massive growth, success, and increased income in a short period of time.

I understand the resistance to adopt new ways of working, Even the biggest A-players tend to avoid things they don't feel 100% comfortable with, but to become a millionaire you often have to lean into the heat and take even more action when you feel uncomfortable.

The principle is actually very simple. Start looking forwards not backward. Work on a budget for your life or business. In order to do this in a simple way, look at three things; your monthly income (record all sources of income), your monthly expenses (record all expenses), and what's left over (your profit monthly). Document this with paper and pen or on a spreadsheet.

Once you have the month planned project the next 12 months ahead. This will get you looking forwards not backward and help you to see the future from a financial perspective.

What happens if you don't like what you see?

Well, that's a good thing, because you are looking forward which means you can change things.

Ask yourself new questions based on looking into the future.

1. How can I increase income by adding new income streams/product services/ added value to role etc?

2. What expenses are not helping me to grow?

3. If I want to change the profit (what I have left) what do I need to do to impact this?

4. How can I re-invest the profit I have left into my growth?

5. If I want a different future, what can I change right now that could impact the result?

Most businesses only ever look backward. This simple exercise in budgeting projection will give you control and help you head off any problems.

Richard often called himself my business Dad, as he was much older than me and was at the end of his career, whilst I was at the beginning. He also introduced me to many other qualities such as management skills and emotional intelligence which I needed at that point in my career. Had I not had his help, I wouldn't be the person I am today, so I am thankful to him.

And that is the amazing thing about mentoring. I continually pass forward the lessons he taught me.

The £2 million pounds he raised allowed us to fund the part-exchanges and grow to a turnover of £13.4m with £750,000 net profit. It transformed the business.

As well as funding, Richard also brought discipline to the business. He was a taskmaster. He was the first one there in the morning and the last to leave. He helped me concentrate. He helped me with ideas. He motivated me. He gave me targets and incentives and the discipline to know that as a young, wealthy person, the business was not my personal piggy bank.

Thanks to his tutelage, I can now look at any business' profit and loss, no matter if it's a beauty business or a recruitment business. I can then dissect that business to assess what it's doing wrong or right and provide a plan for the future.

During the growth period, we experienced after he came on board, we were voted into the 1000 Businesses to Inspire Britain list. We were included in the Sunday Times Fast Track 100 list of the 100 fastest-growing companies in the UK. I was in the media. I was on the covers of newspapers and magazines. People wanted to do business with us. We offered low prices and low monthly payments for cars. Finance companies loved us too because 90% of our clients were buying on finance.

We had 360,000 Facebook followers, which was the largest following in the world at the time for the automotive industry. We were getting 5,000 enquiries a week.

We started to then look at other social media. We started to implement YouTube. We started to use Instagram.

I started to relax a little and enjoy the success. I bought a Ferrari 458. I started to live the life of a successful entrepreneur.

After the £13.4m year, we needed bigger premises to operate from, so we got a new office and showroom in Witham, which was £10,000 a month and had 150 parking spaces. We turned over more the £24m and made £1m profit. We kept growing and needed more funding to keep up with the rapid expansion.

As we looked at the numbers, we realised that we were making more money from part-exchanges than we were from the 'estate agent for cars' model, so before we moved to Witham, we decided to stop the original model and raise more funding to fill the new showroom up with hundreds of cars. Richard raised us another £8m in funding.

Meanwhile, my big passion was marketing. I learned more about it. I invested in courses, training, and mentors. I grew our marketing team to nine people, and I trained them.

We had our sales, we had a strategy, we had marketing. The business was being branded without me even realising it because of the media attention we'd attracted.

I bought a lovely house and went on wonderful holidays. I hired boxes at the O2 and took the staff out. We had a great team and a great culture.

We built the business up to £24.4m and opened two new showrooms. We moved into some high-end cars. I was featured on the Channel Five programme *Million Pound Motors*. This was my first experience of featuring on national TV and something I really enjoyed, all those years ago I had loved drama at school and now I was getting to live it in real life. We filmed in the showrooms for over a month and I loved every minute of it, it was exciting and fun and really lifted the atmosphere. It also boosted the business's visibility.

By the age of 29 I had achieved my goal of becoming a millionaire. I had 120 staff. I met a new partner who went on to become the mother of my child Sammy. I put a £1 million deposit on a £2.1 mansion on the most expensive road in Essex, I felt very successful and was happy in all areas of my life. I had accomplished my goals and been able to achieve more in a decade than most people ever do in a lifetime, yet the next decade was set to be even more interesting.

MILLIONAIRE
SUCCESS SECRETS

- Be bold. When you know something is right, don't take no for an answer.

- Know when to talk and when to listen. When a successful person shares their wisdom, open your ears, not your mouth.

- Begin crunching the numbers, even if it feels premature.

- You may not have all the answers, but someone else does. Seek out experts and mentors to unlock success secrets.

- Understand ROI. Does an investment create income or save you money?

- Understand your margins. Work out the profits on your goods and services.

- Use data wisely. Forecast forward using the numbers.

- Keep track of your performance continually and look for ways to improve your numbers.

1. *The Journey Begins - Starting Out on Success*

2. *My First Office (The One on The Right!)*

3. *What Is Success - The Elements That Create Successful Lives*

4. *With Richard – An Early Business Mentor*

5   Being Photographed for An Industry Magazine

6.   Growing The Team and Having Fun

7.   Enjoying and Celebrating Success

8.   Buying my Dream Home

9. *Making An Impact At One Of My First Events*

10. *Building a Community of Winners*

11. On Stage Interviewing Boxing Champion Floyd Mayweather

12. Speaking At A Conference In America

13. Speaking At A Conference In South Africa

14. Speaking At London ExCel 2016

15. *At home filming for 'Rich House, Poor House'*

16. *With Sarah at my Gold Circle event – forever grateful for the impact you have had on me*

11

Innovation and Focus

People's perceptions of me changed. I got respect from people who thought I was a lost cause when I was younger. Others were jealous, which I now understand but didn't back then.

I was happy at home, and I was happy at work. We were achieving great things. It felt like I was on a mission.

But I was creating a monster. It needed more money, it needed more resources, it needed more of my time, and it took more of my soul.

My relationships suffered. I spent less time with my family and when I was with them, I was preoccupied. I was always busy. My phone never stopped. There were always problems to deal with.

At weekends I'd go into our branches that were underperforming and train up and incentivise the staff.

We got to £33.9m in revenue and I was burning out. I was unhealthy, overweight and stressed. The business always needed more money because we were selling so much. We had so many enquiries. It was voracious.

It was a massive learning curve.

The lesson I learned, and the lesson that transfers to all walks of life was that to stay ahead and to continue to grow, I had to innovate and act on ideas. The company was born out of innovation and needed to continue to innovate in order to expand.

I started learning a lot about innovation and doing things differently and applied what I learned to the business. As an example, December was always our quietest month. So much so that most Decembers I would take several weeks off and go on holiday. But in our third year, Richard turned to me and said: "Adam, we need to have a good December. What are we going to do?" by now Richard knew that if he gave me a challenge, I would typically rise to it.

"December's rubbish. I'm going on holiday," I replied.

But he was adamant and when I thought about it, I realised that there must be an untapped market of people who *would* be interested in buying a car in December, either as a present for someone, or a present for themselves or to fulfil a New Year's resolution to get rid of their old car and get a new one.

In the past, we held some summer events at the main showroom where we invited the community and contacts to a barbecue. They'd always been popular and had generated business. I had the idea to run a winter event and got all the staff together (over 100) for a company-wide brainstorm, which I facilitated.

"We're going to have the best December we've ever had, and we are going to hold an event to attract people to the showroom in order to make that a reality," I explained. "I want your ideas about what we are going to do. I want all of your ideas and want to learn from you. Any idea is a good idea."

I truly believe this last part, because when people know that their idea will not be scoffed at and discounted, they have the confidence to get involved.

The staff started throwing ideas at me.

"We should do a Winter Wonderland type event because that's where people go before Christmas."

"We could get reindeer here and kids can come and see them."

"We could get snow machines and one of those giant inflatable snow globes in the showroom."

"We could clear out the showroom and turn it into a skating rink."

"We could give away mince pies and mulled wine."

"We should put a Santa's grotto in the showroom and people can come see Santa and get a free gift."

"We could have a North Pole post box so kids can post letters to Santa from the showroom."

"We should get owls."

"We should get the *Frozen* cast here."

"We should have a choir."

"We could get a fire-eater."

We ended up doing all of it!

We held a massive Winter Wonderland event with a Santa's Grotto, an ice-skating rink, a choir and all the rest of it and we invited all the local businesses to have stalls. We put up massive marquees and 5,000 people came. The event was so big it made all the newspapers. We had a queue of a thousand people waiting to see Santa and we gave them all a free present. We used social media, where we were bigger than Rolls Royce and BMW, to cover everything, and we ended up selling thousands of cars over that single weekend.

It was a triumph of innovation. No car showroom had ever done anything on that scale before.

We went from strength to strength. The company was recognised by the London Stock Exchange for three years running as one of the Top 1000 Companies to Inspire Britain. I bought some of the commercial properties. We ended up with five locations.

Years before I used to sit on the sales row in Ford and tell my colleagues that one day I was going to be a millionaire. I sounded like a nineteen-year-old Del Trotter and they laughed at me. By the age of thirty, I'd made that dream a reality. But at what cost?

Success isn't easy and the path to success is not a gradual linear progression. It is full of peaks and troughs. The more prepared you are, the more you can level out the undulations, but one of the inevitable lessons you learn when you set off on a quest for success is that failure will always play a part.

As I built my car sales empire, I learned important lessons and I faced considerable challenges along the way. In business the challenges you face are not always going to be directly related to your work because life consists of interlocking elements such as work, family, health and relationships. These all affect each other, so you may be smashing it at work when a sudden health issue affects your performance and takes you out of the game, for example.

One of the key lessons I teach my students now is that unless you can pre-empt the future, there's not much point in having rigid five-or ten-year plans. A lot happens in a decade. People get divorced, people have children, people move away, priorities change; you could get hit by a bus. Your goal today is unlikely to be your goal in ten years' time, or maybe even five years.

For example, maybe you start working in a job and you set yourself the target of being a senior manager in five years. There's a strong chance that after three years you'll be itching to move on somewhere else. The world is chaotic, especially now. Changes happen which are outside our control. The Covid-19 pandemic proved this, as did Brexit. Both those events meant millions of people had to re-evaluate their life plans.

My advice is always to set annual goals. By this time next year, I must start my business. By this time next year, I must achieve that promotion. You can still move towards a long-term goal, but by doing it in annual increments, you can see change and achieve success in a more realistic and flexible way, leaving yourself freedom to change your goals as your life changes. What that means is that on January 1st every year, it all resets to zero and you start the New Year with a clean slate and a fresh idea of what you're going to accomplish that year. The strategy allows you continue to stack successes year on year, you become successful every year, rather than once every five or ten years.

My initial goal when I started the car business was very simple: get some clients. Once I had clients the goal was to serve them. That was a plan. Following my struggles at Big Financial, I was not planning too far ahead. The aim was to build over time. Ultimately the momentum developed at a fast pace but initially I wanted to make sure the concept worked and was sustainable.

The rate of growth and the turnover progression – up to £40m within a decade – belies the fact that there were plenty of challenges along the way. There were lots of things I struggled with from a business perspective and also a lot of things that affected me on a personal level.

My mentors and coaches helped me to make that change and I am grateful to everyone who made an impact on me on that journey. The way I view mentoring and coaching is simple, the lessons you pay for last you the course of your lifetime not just the months you are working with that person.

At 30 I wasn't the person I was at 20, and as I write this at 40 I am not the person I was at 30. Change isn't a bad thing. How you change is how you succeed.

Thankfully, I have had supportive people in my life. As I was growing my car business, I had a few different relationships. Initially, at the early stages of the business, I was in a relationship with a girl called Hannah. She had a lovely family and came from a good home. I looked up to her father, Barry, who was very wealthy but humble and understated. He was a refined man who looked after his family, and he was someone I aspired to be like. He seemed to take everything in his stride and never seemed stressed. He worked in the City of London and was very successful. As I got to know him better, I respected him more and more. I was with Hannah for about three and a half years, and I loved her family. But ultimately the relationship didn't work because I was obsessed with succeeding and with the business and she wanted to settle down and start a family. My obsession ruined the relationship. I didn't pay attention.

When my relationship with Hannah ended in 2014 I went to see my cousin in Singapore for a break. The day I got back, I went out for a drink with a friend, Sean. We went to a local pub where I immediately noticed a girl behind the bar, who I thought was stunning. We started talking and there was a spark between us. We arranged to meet up for a drink and something to eat and became a couple.

I fell for her, and the relationship blossomed. Things moved fast. We moved in together within a couple of months and after six months, she fell pregnant with Sammy. It was all very quick. He was unplanned, but not unwelcome. He hadn't been in my year plan!

Sammy was born in November that year and I turned into a family man. Fatherhood changed me a great deal. I went through a transition and felt I was leaving the old me behind. The partying, the drinking, the going out, they just didn't seem important anymore. Fatherhood was the final nail in the coffin for my old life. It provided me with stability.

Sammy was always well looked after while my focus was on work. We cultivated a family dynamic that flourished beautifully for an extended period. She was encouraging about the business, and she understood me.

Success opens many doors and leads to opportunities. I was invited on radio shows and interviewed. My social media profile exploded as social media grew. My reputation went well beyond Essex, and I was frequently contacted by budding entrepreneurs who wanted advice. People knew me as one of the UK's youngest business tycoons and I was approached by the organiser of a motivational business conference with an offer that changed my life.

In 2016 I was invited to speak at a large event in the ExCel exhibition centre in London. This event was a regular seminar held in different locations around the world which brings together top global achievers who share their knowledge and help motivate like-minded learners and innovators to pursue the strategies, processes and mindset needed to succeed in the business environment.

The events have been attended by hundreds of thousands of people over the years and speakers have included Anthony Robbins and Russell Brand.

The organisers noticed the stories about me and wanted me to join the event and speak to the audience of 2,000 eager listeners about my journey, the story of my business and my social media strategy. Talking to people about whatever it is you are trying to sell, whether it's a product, a service or you, is one of the keys to success.

As I've said before, the more people you can reach, the more chance of success you'll have, which is why I was an early adopter of social media—I could see the potential to reach a bigger audience than any advertising could deliver. With this information at the forefront of my business strategy, I jumped at the chance to speak at this event.

I won't lie, I was nervous, and I wasn't great. I had prepared a few lines in my head and knew roughly what I was going to say but I hadn't practiced, and I had never had any formal communication skills training. I had never even done public speaking before. The biggest audience I'd addressed was 100 of my staff at meetings within the business, and I knew most of them. This was very different. There were 2,000 strangers and a big stage with a panel of people, several of whom were experienced speakers.

However, despite the nerves and the shaky delivery, I loved it. And the audience loved it too. I explained the story of the Christmas event we'd held and spoke about the power of social media and how my company had managed to make Facebook our main marketing route when we launched. The sound of 2,000 people cheering after I'd finished speaking gave me an adrenaline buzz unlike anything I'd experienced before and from that moment, I was hooked.

At the event, I met an American man who described himself as a wealth and business coach and entrepreneur. He is a motivational speaker and a slick talker who had the crowd eating out of his hand. He had some great ideas and content, and we got talking. He also ran similar seminars and conferences around the world and asked me if I'd like to go and speak at one of his events in South Africa.

It was another amazing opportunity that I didn't want to miss, so I agreed. A few months later, I found myself at a conference centre in Johannesburg before another packed room telling the story of my rise to success.

After that, he made me another offer. He was staging several business seminars in the US. How would I like to appear at them?

I was loving this new line of business and was jetting off regularly. But all the while I was also trying to run my business and be a father. I had 120 staff across five sites and a £40m turnover and was now away several weeks at a time, speaking all over the world.

Things were changing for me and the more I got to know about the world of coaching and speaking, the more I realised that maybe that's where my future lay. Top speakers earned millions. They coached, mentored, and helped create success. I worked long hard hours at the car business shouldering incredible stresses. It took a massive financial investment to make a profit. The business was cash-hungry and in order to keep the wheel turning, it needed to be fed large amounts of money. Meanwhile, the world of coaching seemed light, agile, and more profitable. My head was being turned.

I started to consider setting up my own events business.

This ambition didn't go down well with my family or my colleagues, or Sammy's Mum. She liked the car business and wasn't so keen on me being an international speaker. This caused some friction.

Around this time, in 2017 when Sammy was three, he was diagnosed with autism, the diagnosis hit me like a ton of bricks. I didn't have the information and I didn't understand what it meant. We started to learn what it meant and how we could make his life easier. We put a lot of time and effort into putting strategies in place for him and he is a wonderful child. But in those early days, it was difficult. I loved Sammy more than anything in the world and it worried me sick. This did affect my relationships, which also wasn't helped by my traveling and my focus on the car business.

Looking back now, it's easy to see where things started to go wrong. One of the lessons I teach my students is focus. Have one business, or one area that you want to improve and focus on that. Don't try to do lots of things at once. Do one thing, get good at that and then move on. I learned that lesson because I didn't have focus. I was juggling too much, and I thought I could succeed at it all. I'd bitten off more than I could chew. I was managing a £1m a week cash flow, staff problems, fundraising issues, personal guarantees, speaking all over the world, having a family. It was just too much. I put on weight. I became unhealthy. I was stressed. I kept trying. I constantly motivated myself to just keep going. I felt drained but I kept punching through in the hope that things would get easier. *You can do it*, I told myself.

But I was taking my eye off the ball. My ambitions had started to change. I wanted to be a speaker. I fell out of I love with the car business.

My conversion to the wonders of the world of speaking reminded me of how it felt when I started my job at Powerhouse. Back then I felt like I had found a new world full of possibility. Now I had found a new world of coaching and training, helping others and guiding them. I felt it was what I was meant to do. It was intoxicating.

The more speaking I did, the better I became. *This is what I'm best at*, I thought to myself. *This is me, not sitting in board meetings, not looking at Excel spreadsheets and predicting cash flow.* I'd found this thing that I loved, and the irony was, people weren't on board. My finance director Richard wasn't on board and my staff couldn't understand why I wasn't there in the office all the time. I was pulling in a direction that everyone was advising me not to go in.

At this stage, I had bought a big house with land for over £2m. I had any car I wanted. I was very wealthy. I had investments. Maybe having achieved all that, I was ready to move on and that is what I should have done rather than trying to do it all.

I had a vision for the training business, and I set up Big Business Events, which was a small affair, but it was where I wanted my future to be. Enthusiasm for the car business waned. It didn't drive me anymore. It didn't interest me anymore, frankly, because I had a new vision, and that new vision was my events business and helping people, having fun, and enjoying it.

I was invited by the American coach to interview some of the speakers at his events. He would warm up the audience and introduce the keynote speaker and I would come out and sit with the speaker asking a question. The calibre of people he paid to appear at his events was incredible. I found myself sharing a stage with John Travolta, 50 Cent, Al Pacino, Floyd Mayweather. I was living a life I could have only dreamed about ten years previously.

As my attention span stretched between the car business, Big Business Events and the speaking engagements I was being invited to around the world, I made the decision to put a management team in to run the car company. This would hopefully free me up to concentrate more on my other venture. But in hindsight this wasn't a good idea. The thing that grew my business in the first place and kept it growing was innovation. It was built on new ideas that I had learned from people all over the world and implemented from other industries. When I stepped away from the business, that strategy died.

The management team knew how to run a car business, but this business wasn't really a car business. It was a marketing business.

Performance started to dip and because it was such a capital-intensive operation that required regular cash input from investors, some funders started to get a little nervous. It was also a brand very much tied to me and my personal brand. Me and the car business were symbiotic and when finance partners saw that I was building another business, it made them anxious.

I realised things were slipping and mistakes were made when I was not present. I decided to put everything else on hold to go and fix the issues in the business. I was confident I could.

But it was too late, and we started to lose financiers, who are risk-averse, so when one pulls out, they all fall like dominos.

The car business had been built by raising stock funding via partners and the partners believed in me, so they were willing to give the company millions of pounds. Richard got me the original funding and after I had repaid that and proved the viability of the business model, it was easy to get other funders to invest. They were enthused by the performance of the business. They thought it was amazing.

But as soon as things started to slow, one of our funders, which was a £2-million lender, pulled out. The money was needed in order for us to buy stock. We needed a constant turnaround in order to stay competitive. After the first lender pulled out, another one found out and called me in for a meeting.

"We're not going to pull out," they explained, "but we are going to freeze our finance and let you repay it."

"If you freeze, I've got no way of buying cars," I said.

Not only that, but I also had to fill a £2m hole left when the first lender pulled out. The only way to do that was to sell all the stock and without funds, I couldn't replace it. The business was in a stranglehold.

We went from having £8m worth of stock to £4m. We started to lose money because we couldn't buy cars to replace the ones we sold. All the while we still had overheads to service. Eventually, I had to do what any business owner would do in the same situation. I had no choice but to close a site and make people redundant. It pained me enormously to do it and I tried to mitigate the impact as much as possible, hoping that it would send a message to the funders that everything was being dealt with. Instead of looking at the action as being responsible, they panicked further and started to take more money out.

At that stage I had options. I could have sold the business and I had a buyer who wanted it for the marketing machine. I also had a finance company interested in it. I started to attend meetings with Richard and a venture capitalist friend Peter, where we looked at these options to sell.

I was offered a deal to sell it to a company that would release enough money back into the business to stabilise it, which would allow us to rebuild and grow it again with the same process.

But the deal would have meant me reducing my ownership to what would have effectively been 30%. They were going to pay me £100,000 a year to run the company as CEO. But there was a caveat. I would not be allowed to run any other business other than this business. It seemed they understood the concept of focus. And it was a ten-year plan. It was unfeasible. I couldn't imagine myself doing that for the next decade. Mentally I had checked out. My heart was in events.

I was getting advice from every corner. Someone suggested we could phoenix the company, which means closing it, and reopening.

I started to worry about my reputation. I was set on being a speaker and coach but that very much depended on my reputation as a successful entrepreneur. How would a closed business affect that?

I struggled for months, tortured by the decisions I had to make but eventually I made the decision to sell the stock and close the business.

It took ten years to build the car business and six months for it to fail. There was no large pay day for me at the end of the road. I sold the stock down. I repaid as many of the lenders as I possibly could and got the business down to zero stock, much to the dismay of my finance director and of everyone except me.

The reality is that it didn't have to end that way. If I had been smarter, or maybe even more experienced (because you have to remember, it was my first business), I would have sold it at the right time and I would have moved on to what I wanted to move on to.

Eventually though, I knew that if I didn't close it, it would have caused me financial catastrophe. The route I chose allowed me to come out of the business protecting as many of the lenders, investors, customers, suppliers and staff as I could, with my personal credit intact and the funds to continue.

Of course, I had a choice. I could have invested everything I had into the business and I would have in the blink of an eye if I saw it as my future. I could have taken the deals put in front of me that would have locked me in long term, or I could have walked away from a decade's worth of work with a healthy cheque. Instead, I decided to pay the personal guarantees I had and close the business.

People thought I was crazy, but I just wasn't happy anymore. Many people make decisions based on the past. For me, it was a decision based on the future.

The last 10 years had been a wild ride and I had learned so much but I wanted to focus on the next 10 years. I also wanted more time with my family. I didn't want to manage a million pound a week cashflow anymore or have the stress of dealing with constant meetings with finance companies, a few of which burned me when I needed their support, despite making them millions in profits over the years.

It was incredibly stressful, and it was a scary decision to make.

Another piece of advice that I give is that you've got two choices in life when it comes to success. You've got fear or you've got success. You cannot have both. You have to choose which one you want. Are you going to say goodbye to the fear or are you going to say goodbye to the success?

I will not lie. I had plenty of fear at that time. I was worried about starting over, I was worried about what others would think and about going against what my advisors were telling me. I worried about my reputation. I was concerned for my staff. I was worried about having to repay £1m in personal guarantees and losing a large chunk of what I had left. But I was resolute about the direction I wanted to go in. I was about to start a new chapter in my life and put my focus into what I felt would, in the long-term, give me a better life, a better balance, and make me happier. I had every reason to take an easier route and stay in the same lane, but I decided not to, partly because I had confidence in myself and partly because I could not imagine another decade of running the car business. I made the decision, and that part of my journey was over.

MILLIONAIRE

SUCCESS SECRETS

- You have two choices in life – success or fear – you can't have both.
- Keep an eye on the other things in life – family, friends, and health.
- Think and change continually. Embrace change and look for opportunities.
- Invite ideas and creativity. No idea is a bad idea.
- Set annual goals to achieve success incrementally. Don't look too far into the future. Accept there are things you can't change.
- Don't dwell on failure but learn from it.
- Take opportunities when they present themselves.
- Focus on one business at a time.
- Understand when to stop, when to walk away and when to sell.
- We either find a way or make a way.
- Success comes in increments.

12

Make Friends with Failure, and Other Lessons

The decision made been made. I was preparing to exit, however further problems with the business developed throughout December 2017, which made Christmas difficult for me and for all the staff, who were concerned about their jobs. We struggled on through the festive season because I wanted them to have jobs through Christmas.

I was miserable and I didn't give Sammy or my family a good Christmas or New Year. I was difficult to live with for a while and I will admit I felt sorry for myself.

In the New Year, I almost thought there was an escape route. A new buyer expressed interest and the deal looked favourable. In early January I had several meetings with a large finance company that wanted to purchase the business without holding me hostage for the next decade, which was an ideal scenario.

The deal looked close and my spirits lifted. It would save me £1m personally, my team would keep their jobs and it would keep the suppliers happy. I fought for it hard and I believed that Midas touch was back. I found renewed energy. We had three meetings. I went to London to see the CEO of this very large financial institution to get our offer, only to be told the chairman had blocked the offer.

I cannot begin to describe how hard that conversation hit me. It had been a roller coaster and I was shattered.

But I picked myself up again and, Peter who had been helping me at that crucial stage of the business, explained to me before I pulled the plug that I had to go and visit the partners personally and tell them. It was incredibly daunting and it all started to feel very real, our partners at this stage were large finance companies and I had to explain to them my decision, one of them had stood by me and two of them frankly had created the situation I was finding myself in.

What happened next shocked me to my core! I plucked up the courage, went in and informed them of my next move which was essentially going to be my last one.

What do you think they said?

"You can't close it. It's too big. We'll think about releasing some funds." They talked about reopening the business again and restructuring. All these new potential options came out of the woodwork.

"We want to support you," they said. It messed with my head because I'd made the decision and if they really *did* want to support me, surely, they wouldn't have pulled out in the first place. These were people I'd had close business relationships with.

The meetings and discussions dragged on for a few more months and drained me more. I had to jump through hundreds of hoops to keep the people happy who had essentially destroyed me.

I wanted to lose my rag with them, I want to move on, and I was stuck in purgatory. The indecision from the financial companies made it worse. The reality was that they had zero interest in helping me. They just didn't want the decision to close the business being made before they could swoop in and pick the bones.

I can honestly say during that six months of hell I learned more than I have ever learned in any period of success.

It made me a better businessperson in the future because I have been able to help many entrepreneurs who may have found themselves in similar difficult, painful places and help them learn from what I went through.

Despite the empty promises, it was over, and I did my very, very best to minimise the damage, but it just wasn't possible to pay up everyone because too many funders pulled out. There was not enough money left. When it was all finished some people lost money and I apologise for that. But the people that did lose money had been working with the business for many years and had made plenty through us.

I wasn't able to pay everyone personally and I gave over one million pounds in personal guarantees. I did also pay the staff wages personally during that period. When the business closed, I moped around the house like a bear with a sore head for a week. I'd just spent a decade building something incredible and within six months, it had gone.

However once everything was done, I started to feel a sense of relief, which is strange to say. I started to look to the future. I was finally able to get excited again. I hadn't been able to give my full focus to the speaking and coaching business and with the car business gone I had the most precious asset back in my life, which was time.

I already had some coaching clients and on Monday I got myself up, put on a suit and went to work in the tiny office where my events business was located. I had three staff. I was down, but I was not out.

I got my head straight and focused on the next part of my journey which was to create the UK's best coaching and mentoring company, and to then expand globally. And that's what I turned all my attention and all my dedication and focus towards.

If you want to be successful, you must accept that things are not always going to go the way that you want them to go. But for you to continue rising, you have to keep moving forward anyway.

The lessons I learned over that hard period were profound and vital for success and in the rest of this chapter I will share them with you.

Do what you love

I believe that you only live once. We have one opportunity, and we are only here for a short time, so don't waste it on things that aren't going to work or which you are not committed to. Sometimes that's hard. In relationships for example, inevitably it means someone will get hurt. In careers, it means maybe you have to walk away from the security of a job that you don't enjoy and suffer a period of insecurity. For entrepreneurs, this means letting go of something that you may have once loved and invested time and effort in.

When I made the decision to close the car business, I had reached the right mindset. I knew what I wanted to do and where my heart was, and I didn't want to waste any more time.

Sometimes, when you have a vision or an instinct, you should follow it. If it's a massive diversion from what you've done before, some people will probably doubt you. Sometimes you won't be able to attain your goal. So, realism is important too. For example, if you're forty-five and can't sing but dream about being a pop star, you probably need a reality check. Most people are sensible enough to know the difference between achievable dreams and goals and pie in the sky.

You can choose to listen to naysayers, or you can choose to listen to yourself. When I was thinking about starting my coaching and events business, I used the four stages. I had the right information because I knew how to make money. I knew about the business models and how to coach because I'd been engrossed in that world for years. I had helped other people during my career and had also paid for coaching with others. I'd seen it done. I'd seen that a business could grow. I'd seen it could scale. I needed to take action and by setting up the business had already started to act. Free from the distractions of the car business, I knew I could take consistent action to be persistent and I understood the environment I needed to be in and to develop.

Understand risk

People are understandably nervous about taking risks. What if it goes wrong? What if I fail? Both are valid concerns. However, here's some bad news for the risk averse. If you take risks, you get opportunities. You can't succeed without taking risks. And the only way you learn how to do something is to give it a try. Risk is in the DNA of an entrepreneur. To take the plunge and give something a try, you need to take a risk and if you fail, you still need to take a risk when you try something else. To succeed consistently, embracing risk is key. I've known people who, after facing financial ruin, become extremely cautious. They shy away from any kind of risk. In contrast, I tend to seek out and manage risks effectively. I've had setbacks and in truth have become a little bit less risk-orientated, but I will never shy away from taking a risk if that risk is worth the reward. I'd rather have a go and fail than not have a go at all.

That said, I wouldn't blithely walk into something and take a risk if it was a stupid risk to take. So, how do you gauge intelligent risk? I use a formula I learned from one of my coaches. First, what is the best-case scenario? What is the best outcome you can achieve from taking the risk? What's the best thing that can happen? Then ask yourself what the worst-case scenario or outcome will be from taking the risk. What is the worst thing that can happen? Finally, ask yourself what the most likely outcome or scenario is if you take the risk. Now you have your best-case scenario, your worst-case scenario and your probable outcome. And with this information, you can make an informed decision on whether the risk is worth taking.

For example, when I started Big Business Events, I asked myself what the best-case scenario would be It was that I become one of the best in the industry, famous as a coach and speaker. I made millions of pounds and I featured on TV, maybe as a new Dragon on *Dragon's Den*. I also helped people and I created a legacy. Then I asked myself *what's the very worst thing that can happen?* The worst case would be that I built a small coaching business and maybe it never made millions, maybe it didn't get big, maybe I didn't get to be as successful as I had been. Maybe it failed and didn't work out. Could I handle that? What was the most likely thing to happen? I understood how to grow businesses, I was passionate about this business, and I worked really hard, so the most likely scenario was that I would build a business that was successful.

One caveat to this technique: be completely honest with yourself when you answer these questions.

Focus on one thing

I was successful at turning the car business into a multimillion-dollar company because I was laser-focused on making it work. It consumed me. The failings happened when I started to focus on something else. If my focus had remained on the car business, I have no doubt things would have turned out differently. I take responsibility for that, and I hope that having learned that lesson, I can now help others and guide them in the right way.

Focus requires discipline and discipline is an important attribute in all areas of success. You need discipline to be persistent and to take the right action in your quest for success. Without discipline, it is very easy to falter. In order to maintain self-discipline, it's important to remain aware of why you are doing whatever it is you are doing. It is also important to keep sight of your overall goal and the result you want. Discipline allows you to keep moving towards a result without veering off the path.

Focus also allows you to have an in-depth understanding of what you are doing and where you are in your journey. Consequently, this allows you to review your progress and to correct any mistakes. The ability to self-criticise is important. I am probably my own biggest critic. The ability to recognise when you are doing things wrong can sometimes make a huge difference and stop you from making mistakes.

Focus is more important than intelligence and lack of focus is one of the biggest reasons why people fail. In business I see it happening repeatedly with people who try to focus on too many things. They want to start three businesses at a time and then they're surprised when they fail. It's not that they're stupid. It's just that they didn't focus on one thing at a time. The biggest failing for me was that I didn't focus on Big Cars. I should have focused and then I would have known when to sell the business.

Now I teach clients who have several businesses a tactic to help them choose which ones to focus on. This method also works with other areas of life if you adapt it.

The best way to explain it is to focus on the following specific example.

A client, Kam, explained to me that he had several businesses, but was losing £30,000 a month and didn't know which one to focus on. He was torn. I helped him turn his loss-making portfolio into a £10m-a-year machine. He owned a cemetery, a chauffeur business, a car servicing business, and a finance business.

I asked him for an overview. Which businesses were working? Which were making money? He explained that the chauffeur business was breaking even, the service business was losing money, the finance business was making a little bit of money and the cemetery was making some money but was draining his time. I then asked him to rate how passionate he was about each of the four businesses on a scale of one to ten, with one being the lowest score. The cemetery scored a three—he wasn't that passionate about it. He was very passionate about the service business and gave that a ten. He was also keen on the finance business which scored 8 out 10. The chauffeur business limped in with a two. I then asked him to rate each business on its ability to earn money, again, on a one-to-ten scale. The cemetery business was high on the scale, which he said was the reason he persisted with it; however, it would take ten or fifteen years before it started making a decent return. The chauffeur business scored three and he admitted it was never likely to make considerable profits. Both the service and finance businesses had considerable potential to expand and return healthy profits. With the answers to those questions, I knew that Kam was not passionate about the cemetery. "It's time to walk away from it," I advised. He was also not passionate about chauffeur business, which made no money, so it was time to cut ties with that. The service business and the finance business, however, had synergy; he was passionate about them, and they were potentially profitable, which all indicated they would be the best options for him to focus on. I also encouraged him to entwine them together, and that's what he did. It wasn't rocket science. It was logical. And the problem is, people find it hard to be logical about their businesses because they're emotional about them. Which leads to the next lesson.

Take the emotion out of business

Business is a game. It's an intellectual sport and the person with the best strategies wins. When you start to see it as anything other than a game, you run the risk of bringing emotion into your decision-making process, and emotion has a habit of clouding judgement.

At the beginning of my entrepreneur journey, many people I looked up to told me *it's not personal*. I didn't understand. It was personal to me because it was my business. But that's the wrong way of looking at it because business is a game. If you're playing Monopoly and you start losing, or somebody buys a house and you land on it and have to pay rent, you don't start crying. You don't pick the board up and throw it at a wall. You understand that you are playing a game, and that it's not personal, it's just business. If you're going to play the game of business, don't make it personal and understand that it isn't personal. Every rejection you get is not personal. Every failure - It's not personal. Business doesn't feel sorry for you. Money doesn't feel sorry for you. When you have no money, money isn't somewhere else crying for you. Money doesn't judge and it doesn't care who you are. You know the principles to make money or not make money and if you haven't got any money that's your fault, because you're not doing the right things to make money. You're not adding enough value, creating enough, or giving enough. If you've got no money, you're either being irresponsible with what you spend or you're not creating enough value in what you do to have more of it.

Failure can also be emotive. It can create fear, sadness, regret. These are all understandable reactions to failure, and it is perfectly human to want to curl up in a ball and close yourself off after a failure, as I did after my problems with the car business. However, if you dwell on these negative emotions, it becomes harder to move forward, which is why, a lot of the time, failure kills entrepreneurial spirit.

In order to be successful and cultivate a success-orientated mindset, it is important to be able move on from failure and take the emotion out of it.

In my business, for example, we may sometimes try something that doesn't work, but when we do, we analyse why it didn't work, rectify the problems the next time and move on.

Tomorrow is a new day. Attitude to failure is everything. Learn and move on. Don't take failure personally. Don't take it personally if someone beats you to something, or closes that deal that you thought was yours, or changes their mind about an agreement you had. Look after your own interests because they will be looking after theirs.

Accept defeat like a footballer. Players such as Cristiano Ronaldo don't take defeat personally. He scores in games and when he doesn't score, he analyses why. He looks at what he could have done better and implements that the next time he plays. He's got continued discipline and motivation. And you find that in successful people.

The ability to take emotions out of decisions and view situations objectively will allow you to stop repeating mistakes and to make better, clearer, more logical decisions. For example, I know now that even though I appreciate the potential of Big Business Events and am invested in it as a business, I would be measured enough to sell it if something else came up that I was more interested in developing. I would have the experience to be able to understand that before I go on a new journey, I need to close off old journeys.

Take responsibility

When things go wrong, take responsibility for your mistakes and never look for other people to blame. If it's a mistake made in your business, and you are the person in charge, it is no one else's fault. The buck stops with you. This is hard for some people to understand, but your business functions the way it does because of the way you built it. If someone else makes a mistake, it's your fault because you employed someone with the wrong skill set, or you didn't train someone properly. Mistakes don't happen by accident. When the car business failed, it failed because of me and I owned the failure.

Understand, however, that there is a difference between owning mistakes and beating yourself up unnecessarily about them or bringing yourself down. Understand that everyone makes mistakes and that making mistakes is a way to learn. When I make mistakes, I ask myself questions. What could I have done better? What did I do wrong? If someone I employ makes a mistake, I don't look at it as if my staff made a mistake. I look at it from the perspective that I made a mistake, because I employed the staff, I trained the staff, I told them what to do. It's not their fault. It's my fault.

Be calm. Be understanding. When something goes awry, identify what caused the problem, identify the process that needs to be fixed using the information you have and put in place processes to make sure it doesn't happen again. If you don't put the systems and processes in place, it's your fault if it happens again. What have you missed? What do you need to do differently? Learn the lesson and then work out a strategy to make sure it will not happen again.

Be good to people

When I set up my coaching business it was important that clients understood that we are an organisation that genuinely cares about people. Having experienced many different coaching programs myself over the years, some good, some bad, I felt compelled to create a culture where the client is king.

I also learned this lesson way back in my career at BMW when I had a lightbulb moment and understood that if I cared about my clients, they would care about us, remain loyal and want to do business with me.

Don't be afraid of failure

Failure is temporary. No one fails forever. Failure is a moment in time. Learn, move on. Accept it happened then understand what your next end result will be. What do you want to achieve and work towards?

MILLIONAIRE

SUCCESS SECRETS

- Your most precious asset is time; money can be replenished, but once invested, time is irretrievable.

- Do you love what you do? Give it a score out of 10 – 1 being hate to and 10 being you live and breathe it.

- Assess Your Risks Effectively: Evaluate risks by considering the bad, worst, and most likely scenarios.

- Stay laser-focused and never lose sight of what's working.

- Let go of personal attachments – What's holding you back? Release it and move forward.

- Failure is a moment in life – it doesn't last forever.

13

Coach Party

Earlier, I explained why planning too far ahead can sometimes be futile because life has a habit of taking you down unplanned paths. My diversion into the world of speaking and coaching is a good example of this.

Opportunities arise in life and for the most part, it is worth taking them because they lead to new places, new experiences and new contacts. Often, these opportunities arise seemingly randomly but while they are not always a result of conscious actions you've taken, they usually happen because of some chain of events that you set in motion in the past but haven't even connected in your own mind.

For instance, I got invited to my first speaking engagement because someone had seen me in a magazine or newspaper and had then checked out my carefully curated social media. When I was asked what I could talk about, I realised that the Christmas event I staged after Richard insisted that we did something to boost December sales would provide relevant content, which in turn entertained and enlightened the audience. Their reaction ensured I was offered further opportunities. All the past decisions and actions led to that moment and then influenced what I did in the future. Life takes unexpected twists for sure, but there's usually a logical pattern that leads up to them.

The event at London's ExCel conference centre was a turning point in my life. It was one of those defining experiences that set me off on a new path.

Through that event I met the American coach and it is fair to say that I was impressed. Up to that point I'd seen my fair share of motivational speakers and he was good. He knew how to work a room. He liked me and he could see potential. He ran his own events around the world and earned a fortune from them. He was also a coach and mentor and he offered to train me with his business partner, Damien.

"You're good, but we'll get you even better," he said.

Other opportunities arose and I spoke in the ExCel centre at several times over just a few months. Bearing in mind I'd never spoken publicly before, I approached the first event with supreme confidence, feeling that I wouldn't be nervous. But when I stood on the stage and saw a sea of faces in the audience, my heart started pounding and nerves took hold. For a moment I questioned whether I'd taken on more than I could handle but as a natural risk-taker, I gave myself a quick mental pep talk and launched into my presentation. As I started talking, the fear disappeared. The next time I went back, it got a bit easier and while my heart wasn't racing, I could still feel the adrenaline. I was feeling my way, learning the ropes. I had no speaking or presentation skills. I was thrown in at the deep end and I just did it.

And the truth was, I wasn't very good. But that is the same as everything in life. The first time you do anything challenging, you are generally going to be terrible at it, no matter who you are. This is how we as humans learn. Trial and error. From speaking and walking, to building spaceships, conducting brain surgery and making videos for social media.

When faced with something new and challenging, you have two choices. You can do it, or you can choose not to do it. You can think about it, and you can torture yourself and you can do it in a year's time, but when you do it in a year's time, you'll still most likely be terrible because it will still be the first time you do it. Alternatively, you can do it now, be terrible, get better and be really good in a year's time.

The best option, and the one I advise my clients to go with, is to get the right information needed to tackle the task, suck it up and do it because none of us become masters at anything by not doing that thing. If you do nothing, you get nothing. If you do nothing consistently, you're unlikely to get far. It's only when you do things consistently that you build skills and confidence and grow.

From those London events, I got invited to South Africa, where again I spoke in front of over 2,000 people. At the ExCel there were other people on stage with me. In South Africa, I was on my own and had a fifteen-minute slot.

The event was in Johannesburg and was staged very professionally.

It was explained to me like this: "You're going to go on and speak and you're going to entertain the audience."

I did it and I loved it. The buzz I got from being cheered by an audience of thousands was addictive. It doesn't matter whether you are millionaire and live in a mansion and drive a Ferrari, having an audience cheer you is an amazing experience. I can understand why performers and athletes find it hard to retire. No wonder the Rolling Stones keep touring. None of them needs the money, but I bet they are addicted to the adulation.

In South Africa, I also started to speak with some of the celebrities that were booked to appear at his events. I met a guy called George Ross who was Donald Trump's right-hand man on *The Apprentice* and a former executive vice president and senior counsel of the Trump Organization. I also met Stedman Graham, a famous American educator, author, businessman, and public speaker. He is the long-term partner of Oprah Winfrey. We got on well and chatted several times over the weekend – even going on safari together in Sun City, near Johannesburg. I realized the international motivational seminar circuit offered someone like me – a kid from Essex – access to a different world. I loved being around people I could learn from. It was the perfect environment for high-level success with the perfect source of information.

And although I went down a storm in Johannesburg, I realised that I was not a master by any stretch of the imagination. And that's when I started committing to working on improving myself in this new endeavour and studying it to become better. It became my new thing. I wanted to be a great speaker. I wanted to be the best and it became my obsession.

I wanted the information. I put myself in the environment. I took action and I was persistent. I went on this journey to learn. I got some coaching and speaker training, and I spoke at several more events, largely in the US.

After South Africa, I went to Orlando where I was given opportunities to interview incredibly famous people. It was a difficult decision because it meant I was away on Sammy's birthday. I was conflicted about whether to go, but I knew it was a route to more opportunity and a better future for the family, so I agreed.

Once there, I interviewed John Travolta, 50 Cent, Calvin Klein, Fredrik Eklund and Randi Zuckerberg, who is Mark Zuckerberg's sister. I met all these amazing people. I then flew with John Travolta to LA where I hosted a whole event with Al Pacino. Each of the celebrities was getting around a quarter of a million to half a million dollars to be at the event and several students, including me, were invited up to ask individual questions. The budgets for these events were huge but from 2,000 delegates, it was possible to sell many £25,000 coaching programmes and make a profit of several million dollars.

It was big money and while my car dealership was doing okay at the time, my head was turning as I questioned whether I'd rather be in Essex selling second-hand cars or out in LA with Al Pacino.

At each event, I also got to talk about business and the process of business creation.

The American coach showed me how you can take someone, teach them, and turn them into a megastar. He had the ability to do that by giving them access to the star-studded environments he created.

After the events, I posted details of the people I'd met on my social media, and I started to get my own clients by using social media as my shop window. People could see the results I was getting, and they started to approach me in the hope that I'd share the secrets of success with them, allowing them to be successful too. The enquiries predominantly came from SME owners who had established their businesses and wanted to move up to the next level. Some were stale and needed that extra push and expert information that would ignite them and allow them to become millionaires. I loved the speaking; I loved the people I was meeting, and I loved the opportunity to share my knowledge and help other people. Consequently, I set up Big Business Events (which ironically was a small enterprise at the beginning, but you've got to dream big).

In the UK, I ran a series of small events that were well attended, largely due to my established profile in Essex. My debut event took place in London, where guests included Patsy, a co-founder of The Business Lounge and Lee McQueen, winner of The Apprentice in 2008 and a subsequent associate of Alan Sugar. Lee has since gone on to establish his own business.

The business model for the events was simple. I rented the space in a hotel or conference centre, booked speakers, promoted the events through social media and sold tickets. For delegates who wanted to explore what I could do for them further, I developed coaching programmes.

It was a great success and I felt like I had found something that I had been searching for over many years because it lit me up. I knew that the system would work and that people would want to sign up to the coaching systems I developed because I put myself in the shoes of potential clients and I knew what they would be looking for.

At Ford and BMW, I yearned for the knowledge I now share. Back then, I needed a guide to navigate through professional development; I was thirsty for the wisdom and strategies I currently offer through my events and programs. After traversing the globe and investing heavily in personal development and coaching, I gained an edge over other coaches and speakers—I didn't just learn; I lived it. Every piece of advice I give is steeped in lived experience, aimed at providing the clear, practical guidance I once sought.

I went on every course money could buy and literally travelled the world to find the level of info I was offering. I invested thousands and got information piecemeal from different sources but never quite found one person or provider that had all the answers I needed in one place.

That was my business offering. I could show people the whole picture. I was living the life of a successful entrepreneur and I was ready to share with the world the information that allowed me to get where I was.

After that first event in London, I signed ten people up on a year's coaching and mentoring programme. Obviously, there was a lot of preparation that went into it, a significant investment and a lot of planning and time commitment for the coaching. There was also the development of my own intellectual property, gained after thousands of pounds of investment that I'd made in my own quest for knowledge and information. However, the business model was impressive. It was easy to see how I could make considerable profits from the endeavour. In relation to the car business, which was complex, cumbersome and cash-hungry, events and coaching was nimble and easily scalable. To put it into perspective, in the car business even earning £1 million-a-year profit required five sites, 120 people and £8 million in funding.

The clients I took on for personal coaching started to introduce some of the methods and ideas in this book, plus others that I share with my Gold Circle members, and they started to see exponential growth in their own businesses and increased success in their lives.

One early client had a £100,000 business. He is now a multimillionaire and has just built a £3m house. Another built his small estate agency to become voted number one in Britain out of

63,000 competitors. There were people like Kam, for example, who had a leasing company that I worked with in the car business. When I met him, he was turning over £400,000 a year. He now has a £10m-a-year business. I was able to help him grow, but also avoid pitfalls.

Later I coached many celebrities and high-level people, for a period of time. Gemma Collins became a client. Joseph from *The Apprentice* came on board too. He hired me as a coach, and I helped him. I also helped many clients who were facing administration or insolvency and have been able to direct them away from trouble.

I had a small group of businesses that were following my advice. I was teaching cutting-edge stuff compared to what was available. I was overdelivering massively. I was giving them very high-level skills. Indeed for some people, it was probably too advanced.

I became skilled in speaking with entrepreneurs and decoding what they said, to learn about their businesses and the challenges they faced. I had a knack of being able to identify the blocks that were holding them back from success.

I am not quite sure where it developed from, experience perhaps but I do have an ability to solve complex problems very quickly.

The easiest clients to work with were the people who knew what they wanted to achieve because I could then decode how they could get there and give them strategies to put in place that would allow them to achieve it.

The process began by defining what each client identified as success. In their introductory coaching session, I question clients about their aims. I explain to them that the process takes twelve months during which time they have all my resources, all my support, my marketing team, my coaches and me.

"What does success in this programme look like to you?" I ask.

Sometimes it takes more time to answer. Sometimes the answer is fluffy and needs to be more defined, in which case we discuss something measurable. Maybe for example they want 82 new clients across the course of the year, or to increase turnover by £150,000. When I know what that definition of success is, I've got my flag in the sand. Then I can give them the strategy to go and be successful.

I don't sell products. I don't sell services. I sell results.

Big Business Events was small-scale while I was involved in the car business and as I mentioned, I had some early successes which showed me how well the business could develop. After the car business closed, I had concerns about my reputation and whether the clients I had would stay with me or not. Some left, but very few, because they saw the huge level of success I was creating for them and others. I was just the person to advise because not only did I have massive success, but I could also now spot the pitfalls.

After the car business closed, I spent the first six months getting the business model right, changing the products, changing the service, changing the message, changing who we helped. It was a period of planning and strategy and putting things in place.

This is essential when running a business. Getting this right laid the foundations for my comeback. I knew the business was going to be an even bigger success because I didn't have to spend a decade learning through trial and error.

I developed products. I created Business Circle, Gold Circle, and Inner Circle coaching levels which clients could pay to be members of and get varying levels of access to me and my expertise. Each program serves a specific client and helps them get a specific result. Business Circle is for those starting out, Gold Circle is for businesses in the growth stage and Inner Circle is for businesses who are ready to scale.

I started doing more events because I had more time. I built the Business Circle programme up, in which members were shown how to build a business from the ground up.

I introduced Gold Circle, which is now a premium £18,000-a-year programme. Members are business owners who I coach and spend a lot of time with. I'm like their own personal business analyst. I help them with all aspects of their marketing, sales, strategy, and planning. Later I added Inner Circle which is A £25,000-per-year programme allowing direct access to me and my team and an unrivalled level of support for the client.

I was a master at marketing. I had a sales process that could serve people. I had a business strategy that created a win for the clients and a win for my business. I knew every detail of the numbers and I knew how to build a brand. With these five elements and my hunger for success, the only thing missing was the team.

As I was making this life-changing transition, Damien, the speaker and coach in the US, announced he was leaving his business partner. We'd kept in touch since our first meeting, and he often expressed a desire to work with me. A long time ago I had paid £25,000 to go on an exclusive coaching event with him in America, which, because of everything going on, I had not been able to attend. With more time on my hands, I went out to America to take this training which was attended by several other high-level performers from all over the world.

I needed to recharge and find my enthusiasm, so I spent a week with Damien and his coaches at his lake house in North Carolina, in which he coached me and helped me change the model I was developing.

He helped me with speaker training and after one event I spoke at, he said to me: "Adam, you are the most dynamic speaker that I have ever seen. You get people excited; you get them to take action." Another delegate told me: "Adam, you're born to do this; you are going to be one of the greats in this business. You've got something special." Those words of encouragement filled me with confidence at a time when I really needed it.

Damien wanted to partner with me but at the time I was still on the American coaches' books.

Back in the UK, we continued tweaking the business offering. We started teaching social media. I found the message that matched the market. People didn't know how to use social media effectively for business and wanted to know how. I was noticing that all people coming to my events wanted was social media expertise. They wanted to know how to use social media to get leads and clients. Previously I had been focused on offering courses and coaching on how to run a business, but people wanted to learn how to get clients using social media.

I had a reputation as a social media pioneer because that was how I grew my own business. I'd sold £40m in the last year of trading through social media and in total, over the years, had generated over £100m in sales through social media, so I knew my stuff. It was a phenomenal achievement. Even the biggest speakers on the circuit couldn't claim that sort of revenue through social channels.

I knew the most successful techniques and strategies inside out. I knew this was one of my considerable strengths and an area where I could rightly claim to be the best in the business, and I also knew there was a demand, so rather than do what I wanted to do, which was to teach people business building, I started marketing myself to help people using social media instead.

I had a brand, and I used my experience. I talked about the fact that I'd done it. I'd been there. And people started to come, they started to listen and very quickly we developed a reputation as a leader.

I created a course called *Social Media Monetisation*. I started by running events in Essex. They were day-long free events in which I took delegates through the dos and don'ts of social media and how to use it for marketing. But the reality was that while I could tell someone what to do, it was much better and more effective to show them and guide them, so I offered a £1,000 three-day course in which they could spend time with my team, bring their laptops and we'd go through everything in a practical, live setting.

My team and I showed them how to run the ads, and how to grow their followings. I had people on the course going from 100 Facebook followers to 10,000 by the end of the third day and getting 200 new leads for their businesses, with very little outgoings apart from the course fee. Delegates were shocked at how much we knew and how quickly I was able to demonstrate the results. I was taking people from unknown to known in three days and getting their businesses up and running on social media. They could see instant, tangible results. We started running free events and they were packed were packed. I booked a room for 80 people in Kensington and a hundred and eighty-six showed up - the £1,000 three-day course sold like crazy. I made £30,000 that night and it only cost me £5,000 in marketing and room hire to get them there. It was obvious how profitable the venture could be.

Then I introduced Gold Circle and I started to offer that too. Initially it was £18,000 for a year's membership. The social media course acted as a feeder for the Gold Circle. Clients came to the free events, and loved what they saw and heard, so they signed up for the social media events, at which they realised just how valuable what I was offering could be for them. This led them to sign up for Gold Circle membership, safe in the knowledge that it would boost their wealth and fulfilment. From every social media course I would get an average of ten Gold Circle members, so I could make £180,000 in a weekend.

I held events all over the country. I went on tour. I went to Birmingham, Manchester, Southampton, Bournemouth, Milton Keynes, Leeds.

Eventually we had our Business Circle, which was £8,000 a year, Gold Circle, £18,000 and the £1,000 course. We had up to 70 people on each social media course. It was extremely lucrative and without the aggravation of the car business with fewer staff and lower overheads. Profit margins were much higher. I turned the business into a multi-million-dollar business in the first year.

As the business grew, Damien, who was watching from afar, got in touch from America again. He had followed our successes online and wanted to take the concept to the US. He offered a partnership. I had the content and the expertise; he had the contacts and the profile stateside.

At that point, he had helped me a lot, but so had the American coach who I felt a loyalty to as he had initially introduced me to this world. I declined Damien's offer.

However, when I got in touch with the American coach it became clear that partnering and working together was not on his agenda. At that early stage there were a few people I could have worked with. They would have done very well working with me but for various reasons choose not to. I started to realise that even though I had owned and ran a £40m-a year business, I was starting from the bottom again in my new venture. I didn't take this personally and just moved on. A few of those people who made that decision back then would be very keen to work with me now. Their loss, as they say.

Damien reached out to me again six months later, and at that time I called the American coach personally, thanked him for everything and informed him I would be working with Damien. It was the right thing to do for me and he took it in his stride. We were never as close after that, but it was a hard conversation that needed to be had.

The reason I tell you this is because, one thing you will notice throughout the book, is that I really do give credit to the mentors and coaches who helped me along the way. A lot of people forget those who helped along the way and even speak badly of them if they parted on bad terms. It is human nature. I am not wired that way. If someone has helped me, I give them the credit for the part they played in my journey. No one creates success alone and anyone who tells you otherwise isn't being straight with you. I am very aware that my transformation from broke to successful is not my work alone and I wouldn't be where I am without the help of all the people I have mentioned in this book.

Working with Damien was a natural match, he had a long-standing deep knowledge of the industry and was able to help me break into America.

He showed me how to become even better. We got 150 people in a room in Houston at our first event. I went on stage and spoke, and I thought I did okay. But backstage afterwards, Damien was worried. I'd signed up about 10% of the room for the social media three-day course; fifteen people at $1,000 a head. Given the costs involved, we had made a small profit, but not enough. The next day we went to San Antonio. I went on stage, I spoke, I did my thing again. We sold about 10% of the room again. Damien took me aside that night and said, "I want you to make these changes." He took apart my presentation and completely changed everything I was doing. He made me delete 90% of my slides.

He then gave me a very powerful piece of advice that I still recount almost every time I speak.

"Adam," he said, "your superpower is the huge amount of knowledge you have accumulated and the speed at which you show people how to get results. Rather than just doing a keynote, I want you to give them a demonstration of power. I want you to show them who you are. I want you to get up and show them what you can do for them.

"If you show that 150 people, what kind of impact you can have on one of them in five minutes, they will all want to work with you, so pull people out of the audience and change their lives. You're the best coach I have ever seen in 25 years of doing this, so show them that and blow their minds. Then I want you to make the offer earlier. I want you to get them more excited."

I followed his advice and at the next event I closed 35% of the room. We then went to Dallas, and I closed 30% of the room again. It turned into a very successful venture and a month later I flew back and repeated the success. I made $250,000 in a weekend.

Next, Damien came to the UK, and we did a massive tour across the country with 300 people at each event, 30% of whom were signing up for our products. It was big, big money. We were on track to do £5 million that year with over £1 million net profit. I brought on more staff to help the people who were signing up.

I built the team. I had the model. Everything was working perfectly. I was officially back and in a very short space of time everything I owed was paid back.

My business life was spectacularly good again and full of promise, I had found my calling, I was transforming hundreds of business people's lives worldwide and I wouldn't have wanted to be anywhere else.

And then Covid happened. Overnight, all events stopped. Damien couldn't get to the UK, I couldn't get to the US. Venues closed. People were worried and scared.

I could no longer do the social media training because of social distancing. I could no longer coach face-to-face because of the lockdown.

By then I had many successful clients. I'd made a lot of money which was in the bank, so my business was in a great position, and I'd certainly learned my lessons from the past. I had low overheads and was on solid ground, but, like so many businesses, I had to adapt to survive. I needed to change the delivery model and go online.

I started to do webinars instead of doing the free events and, like anyone who is in the business of presenting, I found it difficult. The things that made me dynamic, the interaction and engagement with the audience, were impossible to replicate fully in a webinar. My conversion rate went down massively.

But I persisted. I had to get better at webinars, so I did one after the other, sometimes five a week. I worked my socks off. I redefined my model and eventually, we started to grow again.

We built Gold Circle up again and now we've got a brilliant group of people who are all succeeding. We changed our mission. We want to help a thousand businesses to achieve a million pounds each, at which point I would have helped grow £1 billion in revenue. We are on track for that milestone. We have hundreds of Gold Circle members and each month several of them win awards for revenue generated, at which point, we give them an award. They get awards for sales at increments between £100,000 and £10m.

For me now, it's not all about making money for myself. My priorities have changed. I pick my son up from school. I spend quality time with him at the weekend. I'm there for him 100%.

Meanwhile, I'm making other people wealthy. We give them the right mindset and the right marketing skills. We help them develop their message and get the right strategy in place. We teach them how to monitor the numbers and use branding to put the sparkle on top.

Anybody who comes into the programme can be successful if they adopt the lessons and put the strategies in place, it doesn't matter what background they come from. We have clients from local authorities and people who run security businesses.

I love it. It is true fulfilment. People come to me. They need my help. I help them. I don't even look at the money anymore. I don't need to look at the money because I know all I've got to do is help them be successful and then I'll be successful. The more people I help to become successful, the more successful I become.

Despite making the business transition and being happier professionally than I had ever been, my personal life suffered. The separation with Sammy's mum was initially painful for everyone involved.

Now, on reflection, it has worked out better for everyone, despite a difficult early transition. We now have a good relationship and I fully respect her as Sammy's Mum. Sammy is our priority, and I am so proud of him and love spending time with him. He really has been such a blessing.

MILLIONAIRE
SUCCESS SECRETS

- Step up. If you do nothing, you guarantee you'll get nothing. Act now.
- What is the thing you have been putting off, that you know you need to do?
- You don't become an expert without practice.
- Accept that the first time you try something, you may not be good at it. Do it, get it over with, and do it again until you get better.
- Be resilient. Don't give up if you don't get it right the first time. Improve incrementally.
- Seek out successful people.
- Use your contacts and associations to boost your personal brand.
- Start small and test your business proposition.
- Understand what it is you want to achieve and define your proposition. Plan and strategise.
- Think carefully about partnerships.
- Don't sell products or services, sell results.

14

Branding and Social Media

Throughout my business journey I've always tried to be ahead of the game when it comes to ideas and innovation. I was the first person in the UK to utilise Facebook marketing in car sales. I was an early adopter and understood the power of social media. As it grew, I grew with it and implemented social media business strategies that gave me and my businesses a competitive advantage. I share this knowledge and the techniques I've learned with my Gold Circle members today.

One of the key lessons I learned was the importance of branding—not just logos and graphics, but personal branding and the importance of presenting a side of yourself and your business that people can engage with.

After I'd been in the US hanging out with the likes of 50 Cent, Randi Zuckerberg and John Travolta, I naturally started to post content on my social media explaining where I'd been and what I'd been doing.

This had a profound effect on my brand, which previously I'd boosted with regular appearances in newspapers and magazines. My brand was 'young, successful entrepreneur'. When I started posting content about my new A-list contacts, my brand went stellar. I was a 'young, mega-successful entrepreneur who hung out with Hollywood royalty'.

My social media figures went stratospheric, and I became inundated with coaching requests. People wanted to know my secrets and they wanted to work with me.

Celebrity is a funny thing. It's like gold dust. It rubs off on you and everyone wants a sprinkling. I had a waiting list for my £25,000 coaching packages and within a short space of time.

The lesson here is branding. When you start positioning yourself alongside people who are high profile, people consider you to be high profile too.

This works on many levels. Position yourself with successful people, and your brand becomes a success. If you want to build a brand as a fashionista, hang around with fashionable people. And remember to post about it. Social media is your shop window, your TV station, your radio channel. It's the way you broadcast yourself to the world. It is your own personal billboard but it's on all the time and everyone can see it, anywhere.

This idea of branding by association ties into the idea of environment. If you put yourself in the right environment, it influences how people perceive you, which in turn creates your brand. You control your brand through social media and if you do it properly, opportunities come.

I understand that not everyone will have the opportunity to sit down with Al Pacino, but you can control your brand from any level.

The content you place on your social media accounts is vital. If you talk about success, broadcast your success, and celebrate it, you will find that you attract success. Conversely, if you talk about negativity, you attract negativity.

Try this little experiment. Think of a recent success. It could be anything, a promotion, a perfectly baked lemon drizzle cake, a personal best in your HIIT class. Send it out into the world on social media and I can assure you that in general, you'll get positive reactions back. People will be encouraging. Your timeline will start to fill with positive comments. People might tell you about their successes. You may get a few trolls. Ignore them. If you don't feed the trolls, they starve. Your brand—the overall perception you represent to the world, gets a boost of positivity linked to your success.

Now post something negative. Maybe you're upset about something, maybe you feel under the weather and a bit glum. Put that out into the world and watch what happens. It brings back similar negativity. You'll get messages such as, 'you okay hun?' and plenty of others from people who will subconsciously try to trump you with their issues. Your timeline fills up with negativity and that, in turn, creates a negative brand image for you.

I'm certainly not advocating keeping quiet about things that trouble you. Of course, it's important to talk about them; however, it is generally better to confide in people you know and trust, rather than broadcast your problems to the online world. Have the emotional intelligence to understand what to share and where the best places are to go for help if you are feeling low. Friends (the real ones, not the followers) are a good place to start, Twitter isn't.

What you put out, you get back and when you start to curate your social media with the awareness of that process – that like attracts like – you can start to be more strategic about the content you post and show a representation of yourself that promotes success and boosts your brand.

Branding is about how you are positioned in the minds of others, which means that how you present yourself is key. One way of working out how to curate your image is to study the social media habits of people whose brands most align with the version of yourself you want to portray. So, if you're a yoga teacher, have a look and see what the best yoga teachers are talking about, what they are wearing, how they look, how they speak to their audiences. Get some ideas but do not imitate or copy. Be your own version.

I learned a lot about branding from the American coach who was a genius when it came to leveraging celebrity for his own brand.

The power of association works. After my social media feeds filled with photos and videos of me talking to stars, a TV production company approached me to do a TV show called *Rich House, Poor House*, in which I did a house swap with an underprivileged family.

I'd been asked to do the programme several times before, but the timing wasn't right. Now I wanted to take every opportunity I could, and despite my friends and family advising against it, I said yes and was excited at the prospect.

Everyone around me seemed to think it was a bad idea and worried that it would be edited to show me in a bad light. But as someone aware of branding, I wasn't concerned. I know who I am, I am a good person and will always do what I can to help people and even if I did come across badly, what was the worst thing that could happen? A few nasty comments on social media. Someone I know even told me not to do it in case I was persuaded to give the family I swapped with a load of money. Someone else said don't do it, because you don't know who will be sleeping in your bed. I heard every single excuse in the world about why I shouldn't do it, but I didn't listen to a single one. I couldn't understand the mentality of the people who were telling me not to do it.

In fact, when I went in and told the Big Business Events marketing team I was going to do the show they all laughed out loud, everyone thought I was mad. But I knew it was a good opportunity and a chance to get my brand out to a new Channel Five audience and show a different side to my personality. I also knew that once one door opened for TV work, more doors would open.

I remembered how much I enjoyed filming Million Pound Motors. You only live once and you have to give it your best shot and enjoy the journey.

After I told the TV company I would do it I had dinner with my close friends and clients, Steph and Jim, and we watched a few episodes of the show. I'd never seen it and got even more excited. It came at a good time in my life because it gave me the chance to give back.

The experience was not only a lot of fun, I also met and built relationships with some really lovely people. The person I swapped homes with, Kiptieu, had a close network of friends around her who were all lovely people and the film crew who followed me were great fun. My Dad did the show with me and it is fair to say he didn't quite enjoy it as much as I did, but there were many moments that he had a lot of fun too.

I will go into more detail about the show later but I mention here in the context of branding. I was proved to be correct. The day after the show was broadcast, Big Business Events received 2,000 enquiries and we got hundreds of new clients. More importantly, the programme got across my personality.

Branding can work in any area of life you want it to. Perhaps you are single and looking for a partner. Everyone checks everyone else out now on social media so if your brand is positive and you make the best of yourself in the visual content you post, you will attract like-minded people. If you're in the gym and you're looking fit, take photos and post them. Show people that you look after yourself. Physical fitness is an attractive quality and if you're single it would be a good idea to make yourself look attractive.

Being a family person might be considered an attractive quality too. Show yourself with your children.

It's about showing the best side of you. It's about giving the perception of who you are. If you post lots of content of yourself getting drunk and messing around, don't expect people to take you seriously.

Increasingly employers will look at the social media of potential employees and make judgements on suitability based on what they see. It's very rare in any position nowadays where you meet somebody and form any kind of relationship with them, whether that's business or personal, that you don't look them up. It has become part of life.

For me, branding is the perception you put into the marketplace and the marketplace can be for business or it can be for personal use.

One very important thing to remember when you are strategising your personal brand is that you need to be authentic, genuine, and be the best version of yourself. You have to be who you are. Branding is subtle. Be yourself and be the best at it. Don't ever lie or claim you've been somewhere or done something that you haven't because you will get found out. Celebrate your successes without boasting.

People have an innate ability to sniff out BS and they are also generally good at spotting someone who is a fake. If you aren't rich, don't pretend you're rich. If you aren't a family man, don't pretend you're a family man. If you're not fit, don't pretend you're fit. But if you are somebody who loves reading books, you show your books in the background because intelligence is a strong brand indicator.

I make sure that whenever I post something online, I do it as myself. I don't act. I don't exaggerate. What you see on my Instagram account is what you'd see if you met me in the street or attended one of my coaching events. I'm not perfect. I fluff lines sometimes. I occasionally swear. What you see is what you get. But that makes me authentic, and people relate to authenticity.

Social media is certainly a powerful tool, but it is important to remember that it is not the be-all and end-all and a route to riches in itself. Some people spend all of their time and effort trying to build up their followers and increase their engagement in the misguided belief that likes and followers automatically mean money. They do not. As the 2021 Twitch data breach showed, only a tiny fraction of that site's very top streamers were making decent money from the site.

Social media is a piece of the puzzle. In my view, and from the perspective of how it helps your success strategy, social media is the driver of conversations. It allows you to have conversations with more people than you could ever have imagined in pre-Facebook days.

Most people fail in business because they don't talk to enough people about what they do. The more conversations that you have, the more your business will grow. This is very simple and very true. If you tell one person about your business, you get one shot and you're alone in the dark if they don't like it. If you tell ten people about your business, nine of them are unlikely to be interested.

One of them might be. If you tell a million people about your business, and your product, message and brand is right, you can have a ton of clients.

The rule works for all walks of life, not just business. The more people you talk to in the right way about yourself, the more opportunities come your way. Social media helps because through it you can expand the circle of people you have conversations with. And conversations open doors and when one door opens it usually leads to another.

Let's say you're sitting at home, you're on your own. You've got nothing going on in your life. You've got a choice. Put on Netflix and sit there and watch it and go to sleep and repeat again and again. Alternatively, go and put yourself in an environment where you can start having conversations. You might make a new friend. You've opened a new door. That friend might introduce you to someone else. All of a sudden, you're enjoying your life more because you made a different choice.

At Big Business Events we have a 3-day programme that we teach to build businesses, which is called Business Growth Secrets. It shows delegates the steps they need to take to turn their businesses into a machine that consistently brings them profits. On that business machine, step one is mindset, because if your mindset is wrong, are you going to go and market your business on social media? Are you going to go and have conversations? Are you going to do videos on social media? No, you're not. Secondly, you need planning. You need to understand what your vision is. Where do you want to end up? You need to define it and understand what it's going to be. Within that, you need your product, you need your service that you're going to sell plus your pricing and your business model. Step three is conversations. Once one and two are in place, you then need to understand how to speak to more people and get more people to become aware of your offerings, your products, your services. That's where social media comes in. It drives your leads and opportunities and is a mechanism to give brand perception. It gives you the ability to display your message, to display your face, to show people who you are and what you do. It's the most powerful tool for having mass conversations.

It is an incredible piece of technology because by utilising the advertising functions on social media and with a bit of investment, anyone and any business can go from unknown to unforgettable incredibly quickly.

Social media marketing is a skill. There are two games, the organic game and the paid game. While organic marketing is focused on generating traffic to your site over time, inorganic marketing, or paid marketing, uses paid methods to target, reach, engage, and convert audiences quickly.

If you are using social media for business, the first thing to consider is who do you want to serve? Who is the target market for your product or service? Once that is established, get a really good idea of that person in your head. Once you know who that person is, you need them to know who you are. You need them to know that you exist and that you have something to offer. And that's done through several routes but the most effective is through social media. And that can be done either through paid or organic methods.

Paid advertising speeds up the whole process and the key to paid advertising is just one thing: return on investment. That's all that matters. Are you getting a return on investment?

How much would you be willing to pay to deliver the deal you want? That is the only question you need to ask because now the skill is paying for advertising that will deliver that deal to you. The fastest, the most effective way to build wealth for anybody is figuring out how to turn advertising into profit.

Suppose you're selling something for £5,000. How much would you spend to make that sale? Say you decide to spend £1,000 on advertising. From that, you get ten potential buyers, but only one buys. So, you spent £1,000 to earn £5,000. But wait, there's work involved. You could hire someone for £500 to handle sales calls and finalise the deal. Now, your cost is £1,500 for that £5,000 sale. Want to step back entirely? Hire someone else for £2,000 to do everything. Your earnings? £1,500 for a £5,000 sale, without lifting a finger. How often would you want to repeat this? Do it three times in a week and you're earning £4,500. That's a potential £18,000 a month! If you can do that consistently, again and again and again, you'll be a millionaire. That's why I will always pick paid over organic.

Of course, when you use the paid marketing tools on sites, you have to create your message and your content to build comfort, trust and authority with the person you are engaging with. Traffic driven to your pages are leads, so your web assets need to be perfect for what you need them to do.

Different social media platforms have different functions. YouTube, for example, is long-form video and viewers are used to high-quality production. Developing a YouTube channel that will stand out and meet viewer expectations takes time and technical expertise to create content, so I don't use organic YouTube that much but we do run YouTube ads very profitably.

Instagram, on the other hand, is short-form content. I use that more as it provides a better ability to spread messages quickly. Facebook again, is typically short-form content. Podcasts are also long-form but are easier and quicker to produce than video. You can record a podcast on your phone. Podcasts allow you to have a long-form conversation in someone's ear. It is a more intimate form of interaction because you are speaking directly to the listener, often through headphones while they are in the gym or on the way to work. It's just you and them.

All your social media elements should hang together strategically and allow you to expand the number of conversations you are having. The more conversations you have, the more people you naturally encounter and that can lead to working partnerships and relationships, depending on whether you are using your branding for business or personal purposes.

As we all know, not everyone is easy to talk to or get along with and one of the inevitable facts of life is that sometimes we must deal with difficult people or people we don't particularly like.

Believe me, I've had my fair share of run-ins with egomaniacs and people who, in other walks of life, would have been hauled in front of HR. But in life, we have to deal with all sorts of personalities, some of whom can be extreme. Some of the characters I encountered in my early career stood me in good stead for some of the people I encountered later in life, further up the business food chain. The trick I use is to not take anything personally and to also try to find the benefits in people while using a bit of empathy. I might meet someone and think *what a horrible person*, but it helps to ask, *how could I benefit from my interaction with this horrible person?*

I've met multimillionaire alpha males who revel in trying to intimidate. But the truth I tell myself is that these people are just people. They've got to where they have with some skills, obviously, but underneath the bluff and bluster, they're the same as everyone else.

I've discovered that successful people behave differently at different points in their journey. My next-door neighbour, for example, is what I call 'end game' successful. He's made millions. He's retired. He's chilled out, and he's the nicest guy in the world. His name is Kevin. He's a top man. He's where he is because he's done his time, he's worked hard, he's been in stressful environments and now he's enjoying the fruits of his labours. If I want to chat with him and ask him for some advice, he is calm, amicable and friendly. But put Kevin in what I call his 'mid-game' successful period, in the midst of running his business, making big decisions, dealing with stressful situations, and I bet if I wanted advice then, his demeanour would be very different. I would imagine in that scenario Kevin would be a lot less accommodating. Mid-game successful people are busy. They have a ton on their plate. Kevin may well have given me the advice I wanted when he was mid-game successful, but it would have been short and sharp and probably wouldn't have come with a cup of tea and biscuits.

That's what I mean when I talk about empathy. You've got to understand the position someone is in before you take offence or get upset about the way they talk to you.

There's a certain victim culture in which people are quick to judge and get easily upset if they don't get pandered to. But just because someone is a certain way in one situation, it doesn't mean they are like that all the time. Understanding that takes empathy and emotional intelligence.

Building relationships takes effort and some people require more effort than others. Generally, though, if you invest a bit of time and understanding, you reap the benefits further along the road.

I learned this lesson when I was at BMW and one of my colleagues passed me a contact who bought fleet cars for clients. I arranged to go and see this guy and made it my mission to make him like me. I asked around first to find out a bit about him, what was he like, what were his interests. I arranged to meet him at his house and in the end, I spent hours with him. I got to know him well and we even watched *South Park* together in his lounge. He showed me his hot tub and I ended up having dinner with his family because I'd been there all afternoon and through to the evening. He liked me. He became a friend, and I got business from him and from his other contacts. That investment of time paid itself back in about a hundred deals.

Other times I've been offered the opportunity to go into partnership with people. My dad always told me not to have business partners. He gave me a lot of advice over the years, and one thing he said was that business partner relationships always end in tears and that stuck in my subconscious. Consequently, I've not had many business partners. However, I have had a lot of joint-venture relationships, which I prefer. A joint venture relationship is when you are both working towards a common goal, pooling your resources. Typically, this means two companies using their resources to drive a common goal. It doesn't mean that you have a joint company together because having a business partnership and a company together is like a marriage. It's a big, long-term commitment and ties you both down.

Having a joint venture is like being in an open relationship where you are both honest with each other. It may not last forever and as long as there is understanding and trust, you are both free to work with other people. You still have to be committed to doing everything you can together to go and get the result that you both want. This might mean combining both of your marketing resources or sales teams. It might mean that you're going to power up and you're going to be stronger together than you are alone.

An important aspect is trust. If you're going to have a joint venture with anyone you need to trust each other, and everybody has to bring something to the table.

A common mistake a lot of people make when they go into partnerships is that they partner up because they're too afraid to do it alone. I've trained 15,000 people and I've seen it happen repeatedly. They talk to a friend. The friend shows enthusiasm for the idea and then they go and get started. What they very quickly find out is that the friend isn't as enthusiastic as they are, and they end up doing all the work.

To avoid this scenario, I advise anyone contemplating a joint business to ask some basic questions of the person they are setting up the business with. Are they bringing any skills to the table? Are they bringing any specialist knowledge or expertise? Are they bringing any work ethic?

Ask these questions first and answer them honestly and you will avoid a difficult situation where you find yourself driving everything while your friend gets paid for not doing a lot and not adding value. It is a piece of advice that will save many friendships.

If you're going to go into a partnership, you need to have a structure. You need to specify and agree on which partner is responsible for what part of the business. Whose remit is marketing? Who's in control of sales? Who's in charge of customer service? Pick the roles that best suit skill sets. If someone is great at sales but rubbish at finances, it would make sense for them to be sales director, rather than CFO. Everyone needs to understand what bit of the business they are responsible for. Once everyone is in the best role for them, the organisation is the strongest and most effective it can be.

When you are building an organisation and partnering with others, skill sets are very important. There's no point in building a team where everyone is good at the same thing. If you are a marketing genius and you partner up with another marketing genius, all your business will be good at is marketing. There's no point in going and employing two great salespeople because all you'll do is sell loads of products but not have the logistics to get them to the customer and all the customers will be unhappy. A classic example of how two people with different skill sets can create great things is that of the partnership between the founders of Apple, Steve Jobs and Steve Wozniak. Steve Jobs was the visionary and the marketeer. He was the ideas man. He could come up with the concepts and he sold them; he was the charismatic frontman. Steve Wozniak, on the other hand, was the genius backroom engineer who could make these crazy ideas come alive. As individuals, had they not pooled their skill sets, undoubtedly both men would have done very well, but as a combined force, they were world-beating.

MILLIONAIRE
SUCCESS SECRETS

- Optimise your online profiles to showcase the best authentic version of yourself. Amplify your strengths, but always stay truthful.
- Harness the power of social media to foster meaningful connections and ignite productive conversations.
- Extend a helping hand where you can.
- Don't underestimate the power of in-person connections. Prioritise face-to-face interactions to valuable relationships.

15

The Four Stages of Success

At this point in our journey, it is worth recapping on those all-important four stages of success and investigating a little further how, when they are combined, they create the perfect strategy for successful businesses, careers, and lives.

These four stages – specialised information, environment, action, and persistence – can be applied to almost any endeavour you want to be successful at in life. Want to be a successful dancer? You need the right information. You need to know how to perform dance moves. You need to understand the choreography. You need the right environment. You need to go to a dance studio, and you need to meet people and spend time with people who you can gain experience and knowledge from. You need to act. You need to book classes and turn up to them. And you need persistence. You need to practise regularly.

The four-stage theory goes beyond learning new skills or setting up a business. It can be applied to so many areas of life.

For example, maybe you snore, and snoring is affecting the quality of your relationship. This is a common problem and has many adverse impacts. Disrupted sleep is bad for health; tiredness affects performance; couples end up sleeping in separate rooms and resenting each other. Many snorers will assume that's just the way it is and live in denial, making everyone miserable. But there are things that can be done and the first stage in addressing the problem is to look for information. That can be as easy as a Google search to look for products that might help or making an appointment with a GP or expert. Once the right information has been found, the next stage, environment, can relate to several aspects. It could be creating the right sleep environment. Maybe you need special bedding or pillows. Maybe your bedroom isn't ventilated. Or maybe you need to put yourself in the right clinical environment and go and see a specialist. In order to do all of these things you need to take action to address the problem and you need to be persistent because sometimes the solution doesn't appear immediately. You have to do more research or try a few different products before you are successful.

For this four-stage process to work, the very first thing you need to do is to make a commitment to yourself that whatever the endeavour is, you want to be successful at it. You need to commit to success and then follow these four rules.

If you want to start a successful business, get the right information, which might be the right coaching and mentoring, the right industry knowledge, the right legal knowledge, any information that relates to what it is you want to be successful at. Then build the environment or place yourself in the right environment. Go to networking events and seminars that relate to the business you are starting, hang out with people in the same industry, read the relevant trade publications, watch the relevant YouTube videos, listen to podcasts. Then start to take action. Put what you've learned into action. And finally, be persistent, because there will be ups and downs. Follow the steps, however, and you will be successful.

Specialised Information

There is always a way. You just need to find it. The solution inevitably lies in knowledge, or information and this can take many forms. The internet is the biggest library of accessible information imaginable, but it can also be full of misleading information and opinion dressed up as information. My starting point has always been to learn from experts, seeking out the advice of people who have been through what it is I want to achieve and who have been successful at it. I look for people who have done it in the right way or who have made mistakes and then learned from those mistakes to become successful. Learning from mistakes is hard but it is one of the only paths to success. However, if it's possible, it's even better to learn from someone else's mistakes so you don't suffer the same.

Getting your information doesn't necessarily mean you seek out experts for a face-to-face interaction. This isn't always practical or possible. If your aim is to be a successful business tycoon, you're unlikely to get an audience with Richard Branson but you can easily tap into his knowledge by reading his books and watching and listening to interviews he's done.

You also have access to my huge library of success-focused content at *www.adamstottsolutions.com*, where you will find hundreds of audio and video resources.

Learning from others who are qualified to give you the information you need is a good strategy. Seek out people who are successful in the endeavour on which you are embarking. Seek out people in similar situations. Look for experience.

When I first committed to getting fit, I started off by reading up on the subject. I studied some books, I read the *Men's Health* magazine, then, when I joined a gym, I talked to the fittest people there. I asked their advice, and I found a personal trainer who I made sure came recommended from people whose opinions I trusted. Eventually, I worked out what worked for me and what didn't.

A word of caution for when you do seek out information from other people. Remember that advice isn't always subjective. Often, it's offered as opinion, rather than fact. Which is why, in gyms, you'll get three different people telling you three different ways to lose weight.

The quest for knowledge leads to more knowledge. You learn something as a novice and become an expert, as happened to me when I signed up for a social media seminar in America. I knew nothing about the subject but once I started to learn and understand it, I wanted to know and eventually became an expert. Now other people come to me for advice, and I happily give it. Knowledge and expertise are commodities in themselves.

An example of this presented itself recently when a contact called me up with a business idea. Using my knowledge, I was very quickly able to assess his idea and suggest a viable solution.

He was launching this new gym in America and explained that he wanted 250 members in order to break even on his investment. He explained the concept. The gym was going to have an education centre attached which provided free courses and advice on all aspects of fitness and wellness as part of the membership, such as nutrition, exercise, mental health, even business. Personal training would also be included. It would be a community hub and the monthly membership fee was set at $199, which was high but justifiable because of the personal trainers and education centre. When we spoke, the gym had not opened and as a pre-opening marketing plan, my contact was planning to offer potential members a reduced rate of $99 a month for a limited period if they pre-joined. That was his plan to build a member base.

"It won't work," I told him.

"Why?" he asked.

I explained my reason. People will not join a gym that they haven't seen or been to. They don't join gyms off-plan. He hadn't considered this possibility because he was looking at the business from the point of view of a commercial owner. I was looking at it from the point of view of a customer. This illustrates my point from earlier, about subjective and objective knowledge. He was looking at the business subjectively because it was his business, and he was emotionally invested in the idea. He had spent so long designing the concept and developing the customer experience that he knew exactly what the customer would get. But he was so engrossed in the project that he hadn't considered it from the customer's perspective. I looked at the proposition objectively from outside of the picture, while he was very much inside. He could only see what was around him.

"People join a gym because they've seen it. They like it. They like the feel of it. They like the atmosphere and the people who go there. You're trying to sell a community when there's no community established there yet," I explained.

He asked me what I thought would work instead and I gave him my ideas.

First, we established that as soon as he opened there were cost implications because he had staff to pay and overheads to cover. But there were earning opportunities through the catering services provided on-site, which sold high-end food and drink. He needed to get a maximum number of people through the door as soon as the place opened in order to start taking money. But, as we had established, customers were unlikely to commit money to something they'd never experienced.

The key, I explained to him, was to do a pre-launch marketing drive giving away free 30-day memberships on the very first day of opening. Then, he needed to ensure that the promotion ran through January as that's the busiest sign-up period for gyms. The marketing message would be that the gym was the only one in the country giving a month for free in January, when all the other gyms were charging new members. I recommended giving away 5,000 of the free memberships using social media marketing to target 5,000 potential members with the offer.

Around 70% of those targeted would never turn up, which leaves 30%, or 1500 people who will be likely to come through the doors in January, and so spend money on food and drink. When they got through the door, I recommended that staff at the gym sit down with them and do an educational seminar which individually assessed them and then recommend what the gym could provide for them to help them reach their goals. They would get advice about their diet and their exercise regime, and this then would invite them to consider a longer-term relationship with the gym, i.e., a contract membership. One of the key elements of their introductory assessment would be to explain that a large percentage of people who commit to fitness goals as a New Year resolution fail, and then to explain why that happens and how to prevent it. Then the benefits of membership would be laid out. They would learn that a membership is a commitment and that the gym experts would be there to provide guidance and to ensure they were following the best path towards their goals. The benefits would be better health, more energy and an improved standard of well-being. The final part of the strategy I recommended, was to offer a discount to this first cohort after the trial period ends. They would be founder members, which entitled them to a reduced membership fee—around the $99 a month that was first being considered by my friend. Using that strategy, I estimated, he would get more people through the door in the first month and easily get his 250 members at a discounted rate.

When you seek information, you have to be prepared to hear things that you may not want to hear. You may believe you've got it all figured out and then someone who knows better explains why you are wrong. It is not always easy to be told you are wrong. It is human nature to take it personally or to be defensive.

For example, when I first started working at BMW, I was subject to a process called 'mystery shopper'. This is a training technique employed by many businesses, particularly those in the retail sector who pay anonymous researchers to act as customers in their branches. The researchers pose as customers and are sent to specified branches where they interact with the staff as any normal customer would do. They then feedback the experiences to the senior teams in the businesses in order to identify strengths, weaknesses, and areas that could benefit from training or development.

Early on in my career at BMW, the branch I worked in was 'mystery shopped' and the feedback was not good. Indeed, as the manager told it when he called us all in and explained what had happened, it was the worst failure the branch had ever had. No one was identified and no one was admonished. It was just explained that there were a few areas where improvements could be made. I couldn't help thinking that if the same thing had happened in some of the other places I worked in, heads would roll, and people would be humiliated. In this instance, I had a strong notion that I knew who the suspect was. I thought I had messed up in some way. I went and knocked on the manager's door because I wanted to know. I wanted the information in order to act on it.

"I don't know if I'm being stupid, but it wasn't me who got mystery shop, was it?" I asked reluctantly.

"We weren't going to tell you," the manager said, "but as you've asked, yes it was."

I asked him for the details.

"Don't worry about upsetting me," I said, "just be honest."

And he was. He told me that I got the worst score that anyone in the branch had ever been given.

But there were no recriminations or punishments. It was understood that I was a new member of staff and was still at the start of my learning journey. The managers at the branch saw my potential and nurtured me.

My boss explained the problem. The mystery shopper had spoken to me, expressed an interest in buying a car but had acted indecisively. I had failed to develop a relationship with him because I gauged there was no possibility of a sale.

The way the manager described it, I'd given the mystery shopper 'one of those special business cards. The f**k off card'. When I frowned, he explained I'd cut the transaction short by handing the shopper a business card and asking him to get in touch should he decide what he wanted to do, rather than taking the time to talk to him and help him decide.

It wasn't pleasant to hear about my failings and weaknesses but armed with the knowledge of what I'd done wrong, and with the right training and information, I was able to turn a negative situation around and become a success.

Environment

When I was younger, and we lost everything, my environment changed profoundly. The private school was replaced by a rough comprehensive. The lovely, detached house was replaced with a greasy café and a run-down bungalow and the family unit fractured. The comfortable luxury lifestyle was replaced by struggle. Most of my friends from the private school disappeared too. But I continued to hang around with one, a guy called James. He lived in a big house and his dad was a stuntman in James Bond films. The family had a pool, a sauna and steam room, a tennis court and a helipad in their garden, which was about ten acres. I used to go around to his house at the weekends, and it was like going on holiday. At James' house, you could have anything you wanted. They had the best sweets, the best biscuits, the best games consoles and games, the best of everything. And his mum was lovely too.

I remember one Easter at his house. I'd probably got a standard sized Smartie egg; he got one the size of a football from a top-of-the-range chocolatier. Hanging out with James made me realise that when I was older, I wanted to live in that sort of environment, not the environment I went back to after he'd shared some of his massive egg with me.

Throughout the book, I've given examples of how the environment you place yourself in affects how you act and ultimately can determine whether you succeed or not, depending on the other steps you follow. It took me a while to understand this and although I enjoyed hanging out with James at his house, the other circle of friends I had were not so refined. We went out, we caused trouble and as I got older, I spent far too much time and money boozing in dodgy pubs and clubs and acting the fool. Had I remained in that environment, with few good influences, I wouldn't have amounted to much. But as I upgraded my environments, so my success grew. Even the leap from KFC to Powerhouse was profound. Just that seemingly small step up from a fast-food outlet to a retail outlet with a coffee machine and a staff room where I was surrounded by nice things I couldn't afford tripped something in my mind and made me realise that there were better things in life for me if I applied myself.

Your environment has a massive influence on your goals and aspirations.

I think that's why it was such an enriching experience for me when I did the *Rich House, Poor House* TV documentary. The premise of the series is stated as: "Exploring Britain's wealth divide and whether or not money truly can buy happiness, families from opposite ends of the economic spectrum trade lives for seven days. In order to see what life is like on the other side, a family that ranks in the top ten per cent of Britain's wealthiest households trades homes, lifestyles and budgets with a family from the bottom ten per cent. As the experiment progresses the families follow each other's typical spending habits and extra-curricular activities to learn if the grass really is greener."

The idea is a perfect experiment to test how one's environment affects behaviour and aspirations. My house swap was with a lady called Kiptieu and her family. I entered the experiment with my dad, who was living in an annexe at my property at the time. Kiptieu Sheriff had three daughters and her husband had tragically died, leaving her to raise their children alone in South East London. They lived in a two-bedroom flat which was no bigger than my lounge. Kiptieu came to the UK fleeing the war in Sierra Leone.

The experience was life-changing for both of us and also for her kids. When they arrived at my house, where they spent a week, they had never lived in a place with stairs before and it was a novelty for them to be in a house with a top floor. The little girls were running up and down the stairs in wonderment. They couldn't believe the size of the beds. It gave them the opportunity to see that life can offer more, and that, in turn, will give them aspirations as they get older. The experience will influence the children in the same way that hanging out with James when I was younger influenced me. Give people the environment and show them that they can do more and watch their desire to succeed grow.

My involvement in the show had an impact on me too. When I spoke to my dad, initially he was sceptical. He said: 'Adam you can't do that, you spend thousands of pounds on crap every week', which I do, I have to be honest. He said: 'You get takeaways whenever you want and go wherever you want'. Everyone thought it was a bit of a joke. The disparity between my disposable income and Kiptieu's was massive. Her family had £70 a week and she couldn't afford to buy birthday presents for her kids. I had £1600. My friends thought the idea of me living on £70 a week was hilarious.

But when we did the swap, I think I surprised everyone. It was not a problem. I was happy to work to a strict budget and I was perfectly happy living in a council flat. I got to know the neighbours, I got involved in the community. Again, it all came down to the environment. I knew what it was like to struggle.

The flat reminded me of a place I used to live in, so it didn't shock me. The one thing that surprised me was that there were about fifteen locks on the door, which made me realise how insecure the family must have felt. Everybody needs baseline security and a row of locks on your front door suggests that the people living there do not feel secure.

But the people living around Kiptieu were decent, kind people. We had dinner and a bottle of wine with one lovely couple and chatting to them brought home just how difficult everything is when money is short. Every day is a struggle just to get by. I was drinking their wine thinking, *I don't know if they can afford to buy this*, but I didn't want to offend them by offering to pay for it. When money is scarce, there are extra unseen considerations to everything. Parts of the experience reminded me of my own past. I'd been there. It took me back and it made me realise that if I lost everything, I would be able to get back to where I am now because I have the strategy. It would take me a couple of years, but I would do it because you take all the money and the house and business away, but you can't take my experience and my knowledge.

Kiptieu and her family had a real impact on me. Despite raising two children and trying to run her own business, she also managed to do loads of good work for the community. She was doing loads of volunteering for her church, for the local tennis club and for the Sierra Leone charity that she ran. She was struggling to earn money from her catering business, supplying food cooked in her own kitchen to local shops.

She was a great cook and passionate about the food she prepared, and I saw an opportunity for us both. I was determined to help her out but not with a handout. I wanted to give her something sustainable. She deserved a break, and I could see she was a hard worker and ambitious. My main priority was to fulfil my moral obligation to her and the best way I could do that was to offer to go into a joint venture with her. I didn't just want to give her money for her business, I wanted to share my knowledge and expertise with her and pass that to her. I wanted to invest in her and her catering business and mentor her, to show her how to make the endeavour a success.

So that's what I did. I said to her: "Look, we're going to work together on something and if you work really hard, I will support you."

I offered to fund her catering venture and promised to help with marketing, advertising, sales and the company website. The investment allowed Kiptieu to scale up and move to her own commercial kitchen from which we launched the company, Bongo's Kitchen.

We looked at all aspects of her life to work out how to optimise her time so she could devote herself to the endeavour; for example, she spent loads of time on public transport, so we arranged for her to learn to drive. She was delivering all her own orders so we delegated that to a company, which would also allow her to expand her geographic base. We started a branding exercise and created logos. We built a website that allowed people to order, and we started her social media. I funded some cooking equipment for her as well. Even through lockdown, I continued to help and had twice-weekly video calls with her. I helped her with her health and safety application. I helped her set up a bank account for the business.

We had a launch party that was all over social media and within a few weeks of opening, Bongo's Kitchen went from sales of £200 a week to £1,000.

Her income grew to ten times greater than what it was the year before launch.

We'll keep growing the business and reinvest the profits, some of which are donated to her charity, Sheriff Inc18, which helps deprived families in Sierra Leone.

I'm proud to say we have become friends. I talk to her regularly.

The experience made me realise that I love helping people and making an impact. It is my purpose. It inspired me to help more people and the best demonstration of how people can change their lives is if they have the right environment.

Everyone is born the same. We are all helpless babies without knowledge or experience. I don't believe some people are naturally successful while others are not. Ultimately, we are all products of our environments. These can help or can hinder. An adverse environment – a bad environment – doesn't necessarily lead to bad outcomes. Often, being in a bad environment makes someone realise they don't want to be in that environment, so they take action to change. They do whatever they can to change. Other times people in comfortable environments become complacent and lazy. There is a fine balance. The smart part is understanding how your environment is affecting your behaviour.

If you want to be super-successful, if riches and fortune are your things, you should always be aiming for a better environment.

I always strive for the best and this is a lesson I explain to my coaching clients. When you are buying something or going somewhere, don't look at it and ask: 'what should I have?'; ask: 'what is the very best I can have?' Don't settle for average when you deserve the best.

That's why I bought a house on the most expensive road in Essex. I wanted to be at the pinnacle of the Essex environment. I wanted to put myself in that environment. I'm not a billionaire. But if I started hanging out with billionaires in a billionaire environment, I would start to believe it was possible to be a billionaire. Put yourself in an environment that reminds you to continue to be successful.

Action

Nothing happens if you don't act. You can fill yourself with the best information, place yourself in the best environment, but without any action, you will always stay in the same place and success will elude you.

But action needs to happen in the right way. Actions come from decisions and decisions should be made objectively. That means taking the emotion out of your decision-making process and looking at the task you are involved in from a dispassionate viewpoint. This takes practice, particularly when you are emotionally invested in what you are doing, as will inevitably be the case if your task involves building a business or finding a relationship. But in my experience, the best decisions are always made by looking at situations from the outside.

Emotions cloud judgement.

In business when I make decisions about actions, I always try to have the perspective that business is a game and to win you need to be ambitious, strategic and motivated, but not emotional. What happens when you're emotional? You make bad decisions. You make bad choices. When you are in an emotional state, you are generally at your worst and at your weakest.

Emotional decisions are generally made through the extremes of fear, elation, anger, excitement, and other heightened states of mind. If you are at your highest point and you're full of excitement, you make bad choices because you take unnecessary risks. At low points, you can tend to become unnecessarily risk-averse. Decision-making should be a logical game and an intellectual sport. In business the person who plays the game with the best, most objective intellect usually wins.

Business leaders who operate like this often get branded as ruthless. But they just run their operations logically. There are grey areas of course, and sometimes you need to think of how your actions will affect people and what the impact will be on your reputation. A good example of this was when Philip Green took the decision to sell his failing BHS business for £1 after he and his family had collected £586 million in dividends, rental payments and interest on loans during their fifteen-year ownership. The company was left with a massive hole in its pension scheme. He didn't use emotion in the decision to cut the company loose, rather than keeping hold of it and risk the losses infecting other parts of his business empire. As a result, people lost their livelihoods. The reputational blowback was permanently damaging and to a degree ruined his personal brand. But Philip Green is a businessman, and he made a dispassionate business decision.

When you run a business and employ people, inevitably the decisions you make affect their lives. If you are an employee, as the majority of people are, it helps to have an objective perspective on your position within the organisation in which you work. In effect, when you accept a job, you are signing up to your employer's visions and goals and agreeing to take part in their endeavours with a view to achieving those aims. Sometimes the decisions made within that company are beyond your influence or control. Sometimes the decisions made will not please everybody; however, the decisions should be made in the best interests of the organisation as a whole.

Now, once you've made your decision, the next part is the action. And that can be challenging, particularly when the task ahead seems daunting. It's a common character trait to look for reasons not to take action, rather than to find reasons to act. One of the most common reasons is fear of failure and, as I've explained previously, there's a high probability that you will fail at first. No one gets to be an expert first time round. But if you act now and fail early and get the tricky bit out of the way you can learn and succeed quicker. The adage 'don't put off until tomorrow what you can do today' is a cliché, but like a lot of clichés, it is also true.

If a task seems daunting, break it down into smaller chunks and set yourself smaller targets. If, for example, you want to be successful in losing weight, start with the overall vision of reaching a goal weight, find the information you need in order to attain that goal and then break that down into incremental steps. This might be to start by cutting out alcohol three days a week, then four, then five. Maybe then move on to cut out sugar during weekdays and limit your sugar intake over the weekend to a limited amount. A series of smaller achievable steps is a much easier prospect to consider than one big goal.

In order to take action, you need courage and, most importantly, you need motivation.

If you lack motivation, a good starting point is to work out and understand what it is that's making you avoid doing a certain thing. This could be fear of failure or the concern that the ultimate aim seems too big. It could be a lack of confidence or a lack of knowledge.

Once you understand the blockers, you can use the advice I've given in this book to overcome them.

Next, find your focus. Don't try to do too many things at once. Plan your strategy and focus on the steps and stages you need to take to get to where you need to go. Look at success like a journey, broken down into a series of stages. Focus on each stage in order and always have the end destination in mind.

Action doesn't always equal excitement or success. It is important to understand this. To reach your successful destination, you will likely have to travel through some dreary, boring tasks that don't motivate or excite you. This is just part of life and the best way to get through the dull stuff is to keep sight of the rewards at the end of the journey. It also helps to assess the total good/bad balance of your endeavour. If there is more good stuff to do than bad stuff, then overall it will be an enjoyable process.

Always try to remember that to get to the stage where you are ready to act, you have spent time and energy collecting information and building the right environment. You are already invested in the process, and you owe it to yourself to act. If you collect information without using it, you are letting yourself down. I made sure that I took something from every book I read and every seminar and workshop I attended and applied it to my life. Only when you apply knowledge does it give you a return on investment and show its real value. You could read ten books on yoga and watch hours of YouTube tutorials but if you never did a single downward dog, all that time and energy would be pointless.

And when you do start to act, and you see and experience those first little successes that become bigger successes, you create a motivational feedback loop in which the act of acting becomes motivation itself. The more action you take, the more results you'll get. You get rewarded directly for the things you do. It's not always a financial reward. Often, it's about confidence and self-belief. You act, you succeed, and you feel good about yourself, so you act, and you succeed again and so it goes on. Even when you don't succeed, it's possible to remain motivated and to eventually succeed with the last of the four stages.

Persistence

When I went to work at BMW as a young, cocky salesman, I had one goal in mind. I was going to be number one. If you'd have asked me then what success looked like I would have told you simply, being better than James.

James was the number-one salesman on the showroom floor, and I wanted to knock him off his perch. If I'm honest, in my arrogance, I didn't rate him and thought I was better from day one. As I've explained, this wasn't the case.

But not being as good as James drove me mad and beating him to the number-one spot became an obsession.

I did everything I could. I studied. I paid thousands of pounds to attend Anthony Robbins courses. I spoke to the other senior staff there and to the managers.

"What can I do to beat James?" I asked.

It took me months and months of trying and failing. But what kept me focused was persistence. Each month when the sales figures came out and I discovered I was number two again I picked myself up and I persisted.

I worked harder than anybody and eventually I learned that it wasn't necessarily hard work and long hours that were the keys to success, it was working smart. I learned that the secret to James' success lay in the client relationships he'd built with high-profile customers who ordered multiple vehicles at a time and that when his mobile rang, he closed seven sales in one call. I, on the other hand, was trying to grind every person in the showroom and on the phone and picking up single sales each time.

It was only through persistence and the right knowledge that eventually, after a year, I finally beat James. And for the remaining two years I worked at the company it was always neck and neck with me and James swapping places monthly on the leader board. Nevertheless, I persisted in my endeavour.

In that situation, persistence came from a burning desire to prove myself. In life, that's not always a motivational factor. Today my persistence is driven by different factors. In my events business, I am driven to persist by the desire to be the very best speaker that I can and to help as many people as I can. I persist because I understand the value of the knowledge I've accumulated over the years, and I know the transformative power the transference of that knowledge will have and does have on the lives of others. That is the motivation for writing this book. To share the secrets of success and to enable others to have the tools needed to persist in their endeavours.

Persistence is about understanding your goals, understanding the steps you need to take to achieve them and having the mindset and the grit to be able to fail but try again. Persistence builds character and enables individuals to learn, and progress. It's the final stage of the process. Combined, they provide a powerful fool-proof blueprint that can be applied to almost anything in life where the ultimate goal is to succeed. I learned these steps through my own trial and error and formulated them over years. And as I met some of the world's most successful people, I also started to realise that these steps applied to them too. In the next chapter of the book, I'll share some of their success secrets with you.

MILLIONAIRE
SUCCESS SECRETS

The Four stages of success:

1. Specialised Information
   – What are you learning?
2. Environment
   – What do you need to prove?
3. Action
   – What do you need to do?
4. Persistence
   – Where can you be?

16

Lessons from Other People's Success

I've shared the stage with some of the world's most successful people and am lucky enough to have connections that I have built over the years of people who are extremely successful. Every single one has a common trait. They all have professional advisors, coaches, and mentors who have helped them chart their road to success.

They do this for a simple reason. If someone else has already walked the path you are trying to walk, they can share their experiences, show you the pitfalls, and shorten the time it takes you to achieve success.

Here are some other tips from people at the top of their game.

50 Cent

I met the successful rapper and entrepreneur on stage in the US and we shared some banter over my choice of tie.

I'm a massive fan and I knew a bit about his life. He grew up in a poor neighbourhood of Queens, New York. His mother died in a fire when he was eight and he was raised by his grandmother. By the age of twelve, he was a drug dealer. He was jailed for drug dealing in 1994 and he has been shot nine times. Although he had always had ambitions to be a rapper, his life changed when he was discovered by Eminem and Dr Dre who became his mentors.

I asked him how important it is to find great mentors who can provide the environment for success.

He explained: "It is important to find people you respect who have performed better than you have."

He went on to talk about the close relationship he had with Eminem, whose record label he was signed to.

"My first album, *Get Rich or Die Trying*, is the largest selling debuting hip hop album. It sold 13 million copies worldwide. And my head was getting so big it could barely fit through the door," he said.

The thing that kept him grounded was the success of his mentor.

He continued: "The only thing I had to hold on to was that before that, Eminem's album, *The Marshall Mathers LP*, had sold 22 million. I would listen to his record and ask, what is in his record that made 22 million people buy it? He told me my album was the greatest thing ever, but it made me nervous because of how I perceived his album at the time."

And he explained that although technically Eminem was his boss, he was always courteous and treated 50 Cent as an equal.

"Em had a way of asking, 'Could you do me a favour and rap in this song for me?' Even though I was working for him, he always made it comfortable," he said.

Finally, he paid a touching tribute to his mentor by comparing him to his grandmother.

"My grandmother took care of me after my mom passed. She was the person who was there for me consistently throughout my life. You don't know that will meet someone later in your life that can be as consistent as Eminem has been for me in my life and in my career."

John Travolta

The Hollywood film star sat down with me at an event in the US and I told him how I trained a lot of successful people in the UK. I asked him, if he were to coach or mentor a business owner, what would he say to them to help them get to the top of their game?

He talked about ability and gaining the right information.

"Part of gaining an ability is being competent," he said. "You have to have that down; I don't care what profession it is. You must be competent, and you must gain the abilities that are needed to do that skill. That's a primary basic. And if it includes drilling, or studying, or whatever it is, that has to be achieved."

He then spoke about self-belief, confidence and ridding yourself of negativity.

"You have rid yourself of the imagined box," he told me.

He explained the importance of finding the right people to help you reach your success goals.

"You have to ascertain if the person that's giving you help is the right source for that help. You don't go to a policeman to get an insurance policy. You don't go to your mother for help you fix a car, meaning you go to the correct source for your knowledge and in doing so you have a better chance of not absorbing false data about the thing you are trying to achieve."

In our wide-ranging discussion, the *Pulp Fiction* star also advised about setting realistic goals and ambitions.

"You have to make sure that you are realistic in your goals," he said. "If you want to achieve something that, because of your situation, might not be literally possible, don't set out goals that are going to disappoint you."

And finally, he illustrated a point about self-belief with a personal anecdote.

"Get rid of any naysayers or counter intentions, that's very important. When I was a kid, I remember auditioning and some guy that was auditioning me told me to get out of the business. Imagine you are sixteen years old and you are in Manhattan with the wolves and the sharks, and you are putting your heart out there and performing, thinking you are doing a pretty good job –and you probably are – when some naysayer or negative influence decides that you shouldn't be there. You have one of two ways to go. If your innate instinct is to say, 'Oh, they are right, I am nothing', you'll fold. But I was brought up with such support that I wouldn't allow that to influence me. I thought, this guy is nuts, I'm getting out of here. And I went and laughed about it with people. That takes a certain ability to ignore negatives if they are coming from a false perspective, which I thought at the time."

Randi Zuckerberg

When I spent some time in America, I had the opportunity to interview Randi Zuckerberg, the sister of Mark Zuckerberg. She is the former Director of Market Development at Facebook. She played a big role in building the biggest social media platform in the world and is a success in her own right. She is founder and CEO of Zuckerberg Media, Editor -in-Chief of Dot Complication (a digital lifestyle website) and creator of the animated series, *Dot.*

It was amazing to meet her, and I told her the impact Facebook had on my journey to success. Big Cars sold £50 million of stock through the site.

"Kudos to you for using the platform so well," she replied.

One thing I particularly wanted to know from her was the best piece of advice she has ever given her brother.

"That is a great question," she laughed. "When he started Facebook, he was so young. He was eighteen. People were nasty. No one took him seriously in the Bay area. They called him the 'toddler CEO'. He has a really thick skin, but it's hard for that not to get to you. We are only humans. I feel like I've developed a very thick skin but occasionally I still feel human emotions, not totally a robot!

"I read some advice that I passed along to my brother. I said, you are never as good as they say you are, and you are never as bad as they say you are. Don't let the hype get to your head and don't let the negative stuff go to your heart."

Al Pacino

The actor is a genuine legend, and it was an honour to share a stage with him. *The Godfather* series of movies, in which he played the son of a mafia don, are my favourite movies of all time and I was intrigued to know whether he had learned any business lessons from the role he played and whether he had applied any of those lessons to his life.

"No I didn't," he laughed. "I don't really think that way."

I was relieved to discover that he'd never placed a horse's head in the bed of a business rival!

But he did explain that there were things that people could take from the famous films, which were based on the books by Mario Puzo.

"Keep your friends close and your enemies closer, that's a different ball game. There are things throughout it that you learn that are important. Respect is important. Respect who your opponents are and who your friends are," he told me. "And being gracious."

He went on to explain the differences between the character of Don Corleone, played by Marlon Brandon, and the character he played in the movies, Michael Corleone.

"Don Corleone – Marlon Brando – was such an attractive man in terms of how he carried himself and how he dealt with people. He was a person you immediately felt comfortable with. Michael, the character I played, was a little tighter. He wasn't as generous because he didn't come from the old country, and in the old country they brought with them more warmth, more simplicity, even though Marlon's character worked in strange ways. But he was very smart in terms of business.

"Michael never felt that he would go into that world, that racket. He was in the Marines, and he was destined to make his life different than his old man's. Oddly enough the old man wanted him to go into something different, so Michael Corleone had a certain element of disdain for being a gangster. He didn't want to be that, and that's the kind of thing I tried to bring out in the character."

Calvin Klein

For a certain generation of Essex boys, the waistband flash of a pair of Calvin Klein boxer shorts and the waft of Obsession for Men is a signifier of success. So, it was exciting to get the opportunity to meet the fashion designer in the flesh. He's built an iconic brand with genius marketing and advertising. And it was all done with the aid of Kate Moss and some brilliant marketing in the days before the internet.

I wanted to ask him about the importance of marketing and social media and whether he had any idea what marketing tools people should be looking to utilise in the future.

"If I could figure out what marketing would be in the next minutes, it would be great," he joked.

He explained that long-term plans were always at the mercy of uncontrollable change.

"We don't know what changes will happen in the world and marketing is a reflection of what's happening in the world and how you communicate to people. That changes all the time," he told me.

He then reflected on how the internet has helped brands reach new markets quickly.

"We became a global brand before the internet," he said. "That was quite a challenge. With the internet, it is so much easier. You get known. If you do something that is a bit provocative or do something that people are interested in, you have instant recognition globally. We built the global business before all of that, so to know what's going to happen in the next year, five years or longer, I don't know. What I do I know is that the manufacturing business and the fashion business and retail are going through a revolution."

He explained how social media has changed the dynamics of the fashion business. The number of followers now dictate the value of a model.

"What the company has been doing is paying a great deal of attention to social media," he said. "Now, that's the thing. Models are paid according to how many followers they have online, and most people get their information from social. Magazines are practically gone; newspapers are the same. Social media is the source right now of how to communicate to people and I don't see that changing."

Floyd Mayweather

Boxer Floyd Mayweather is not only one of the most successful athletes in history, but he is also a brilliant entrepreneur and businessman. He has turned himself into a billion-dollar global brand and owns a string of businesses. Until his retirement from boxing in 2015, he promoted his own fights and now oversees a business empire that includes a Las Vegas Skate Park, property and a Vegas gym. No wonder his nickname is 'Money'.

I asked him about brand building, and he explained the importance of having the right people around you.

He told me: "We have to try to pick the best people we can pick and put them in certain positions to help us grow. Not everybody is born to be a CEO. Not everyone is born to be a superstar. Whatever position you are in, be the best in that position."

I then asked him how he developed the foresight to stay one step ahead in his business and sport.

He said: "The reason I started Mayweather Promotions was because for so many years the promoters were making more money than the fighters and the fighters were going out there competing. I said, I'm going to get involved. I believe that the talent should get the lion's share. The talent should make more money than the promoter. The promoter isn't taking all the risk and all the chances. After blood, sweat and tears, the fighter should make more money than the promoter."

The audience agreed and applauded him. Floyd went on to explain that when he fought under a promoter, he made up to $8 million per bout. But when he promoted himself, the first match he fought in earned him eight figures.

"How did you focus?" I asked him.

"I bounce ideas with my team," he replied. "Meditating plays a major part in anyone's life. You don't have sit and meditate. You can sit quietly throughout the day sometimes and think about where you want to be at next year. It's all about growth."

He explained the importance of helping others.

"The best advice that I got for boxing was advice that my dad gave to me. He said, "Son, if you want to be in this sport a long time, the less you get hit in any sport the longer you'll last". So, I never really wanted to take punches. In any fight, I had to be smart, because early on I was exposed. I was a heavy hitter; I was a power hitter. Dynamite speed and footwork and ability but you get older and your body changes. So, when my body started to break down on me I knew I was taking punches, but I was still mentally strong and sharp and intelligent. I found a way to beat opponents even though I'm not physically 100%. Mentally I am 100%. I could find a way to get the job done."

Finally, I asked him about his long terms aims and ambitions. What is the next big goal?

"The goal is for my children to do something I didn't do. To go to college and accomplish," he said. "I want them to take it to the next level, for the next Mayweather generation. Another long-term goal is to make sure when I finally retire, I can help everyone around me, my team, to get a business started that they can run and that they are living comfortably."

Anthony Joshua

The British heavyweight explained to me that one of his inspirations was Mike Tyson. Anthony admired Tyson's determination and work ethic.

"I saw that if you train like a champion before you are a champion, you are more likely to become a champion," he said.

And this lesson translates to all areas of life, as he explained.

"Before you become a manager, work as if you are a manager and you'll probably become the manager sooner or later. If the manager asks you to make the tea and you say it's not in your contract to make the tea, you will never progress.

"I saw that in Mike Tyson. He lived the life of a champion before he was a champion. He wasn't saying to himself, I'm not a champion yet, I'm going to go down the easy route. I'm not to run ten miles today because I'm only fighting a novice and doing three rounds. He was running ten miles long before he was doing twelve-round fights, so he was inevitably going to get there."

17

Epilogue: The Success Manifesto

Success is a state of mind. Anthony Joshua alluded to this in the previous chapter when he talked about Mike Tyson. He trained like a champ, even when he wasn't a champ. Developing a success-orientated mindset by using the strategies, tools and techniques I've outlined in this book will set your intentions and focus you on the steps you need to take to achieve success in whatever form you define that to be. The tips and guidelines in this book are transferable and interchangeable. Some will apply to your endeavours, some may not.

Start with your attitude. Don't live with an 'occasional success' mindset. Strive for success in everything you do, whether that's building a business empire or doing the washing up. Do it all to the best of your ability and take pride in your work.

Understand that there will be high points and low points. Celebrate the highs, but don't become arrogant. Learn from the lows, but don't beat yourself up about them. Remain stable in your mentality.

At Big Business Events, I've shared these secrets with our Gold Circle members, and I can say with complete confidence that they work. For example, one client came to me as the head of a £100,000-a-year business. He was working sixteen hours a day as a quantity surveyor and just couldn't break through to that next level. He signed up with me, and I secured him some celebrity branding that he used to boost his social media profile; I put him in the right environment with other successful people. I taught him the four stages of success. Within a year he won the title of Young Entrepreneur of the Year. He became a speaker. His wife won Female Entrepreneur of the Year. He racked up sixteen awards over four years. He started building Premiership footballers' houses before he built his own £3-million house. Now he makes millions of pounds a year.

Another customer had already faced hardship when he signed up to become one of my students. He had formerly been homeless and had managed to turn his life around, find work and then start his own business. He was an inspiration and was obviously motivated and driven. He'd been in an environment that had set his intentions. He wasn't going back there. When he came to one of my events and joined the Golden Circle, he had a digital marketing business that had one client. I took him under my wing and started to coach and mentor him. I gave him training in public speaking and encouraged him to speak at my events, which he did. He started to pick up more contacts, which led to customers. I introduced him to the boxer, Tyson Fury, which gave him some celebrity branding. The business went from that one client to being valued at £1m within the first year. When I met him there was just him and a partner. Within a year, they had a staff of eight. Within two years, he'd secured a massive contract worth £500,000 a year.

I gave another customer who supplied home cleaning products the skills and knowledge that allowed him to secure a contract with a national retailer.

Another client was an Uber driver working sixty hours a week when I met him. He wanted to start a property business, but English was his second language and he had self-limiting beliefs about this. I helped him reprogramme the language he used about himself which told him that he wouldn't succeed. I got him thinking about all the successful people for whom English was a second language and encouraged him to anchor his thought process on them. I helped him with branding and personal image. At last count, he had 32,000 followers on Instagram. He built a property portfolio of £1.4m in 12 months, and also built a £500,000-a-year education business.

At Big Business Events, we have hundreds of success stories just like these.

So where do you start? How do you get from where you are to where you want to be?

Buying this book is a smart first step. The next step is to head over to *www.adamstott.com* where our journey together will continue and where you can find out even more high-level information to help you achieve your millionaire goal.

Another tip that a lot of successful people use is to have a 'North Star'. This is just a gimmicky way of saying have an end goal in mind. Have a destination in mind. Have something to follow so you can set your direction. This will help you find and maintain that all-important focus and will stop the temptation to stray or go off on a tangent that diverts you from your goal. In order to set your North Star, or your destination, you need to know what the goal is. What do you want to achieve? When you know that, you can develop your strategy using the tools and techniques in this book. Get the information you need, find the right environment and start to take the actions you need to take to get yourself closer to that goal. Keep the North Star in sight and focus on where you want to go. This applies to anything you want in life, from a successful business to a relationship or even a new car or holiday. You decide what you want and then you work towards it.

If your goal is business orientated; if you are starting out on a new venture, another piece of advice I give to people at the beginning of their entrepreneur journeys is that at this stage, the one thing you do have is time. You don't have a billion-dollar brand. You don't have massive amounts to spend on advertising and marketing. You don't have the pull or the products or services. But what you do have is time to devote to your idea. The more successful you get, the less time you have, so use this time wisely. Spend more time with potential customers. Spend time learning about your business and making contacts. Time is an investment. Time is the one thing you never get back. You can pump money into a business and get money back. You can lose money but make it back again. But you can never get time back. Once that time has gone, there is no way you can recoup it, so spend it wisely.

Earlier in this book, I gave advice about ideas and how people will handicap themselves by eternally searching for that million-pound idea that no one else has had. People spend so much time searching for it, they never start anything. Ideas are a tiny percentage of the journey. As I wrote earlier, the best way to create a successful venture is to either provide a solution to a problem or improve something that's already there in some way.

One of the most reliable tried and tested ways people have been making fortunes for hundreds of years is through property. Even with ups and downs in the property market, real estate remains an attractive proposition and you'll find that many successful people have some property interests in their portfolios.

For this reason, I would advise those who can, to think about using property as a way of boosting their success.

I bought my first property on the advice of my manager when I worked at Ford. I was nineteen. It was one of the best pieces of advice I was ever given. Having a mortgage at a young age focused me on work and made me think twice about going out every night, drinking and spending money. Financial responsibility is sobering, literally. I struggled to keep up with the payments on the house and all the bills. I took in a lodger. But when I sold my first property, I'd made enough to buy a bigger place. I picked an area and saw one property that needed no work. However, my dad found me another house in the same area that needed a new kitchen, bathroom, carpets and redecoration. He convinced me to buy that one and spend the money and do the work myself.

I learned a lot about property from my dad who used to drive me around when I was young looking at the big houses near where we lived. He told me the best strategy was to buy the worst property in the best area you can afford and do it up. That was drilled into me and it's a strategy I followed several times after my first doer-upper, which, when I sold it, had earned me a decent profit.

Eventually, the equity I made from property allowed me to sell up and invest in my first business.

Without a property, I lived with my mum for a while and then rented. As soon as I could afford it, as Big Cars started to take off, I bought property again. This time it was a beautiful apartment for £250,000 that was part of an old manor house. It had a 20-ft ballroom in it and the ceilings were 15 ft high. Again, it was rundown when I bought it and I put a lot of time and money into modernising it and improving it. I lived there for three years before selling it for £375,000. I bought another house that was battered; this time, a bungalow on four acres in a beautiful area. I got it for £850,000, invested in it and improved it and I sold it for £1.2m.

I've been involved in other property partnerships through the years too, buying and renovating, buying to let, buying properties, splitting plots and developing houses on them. In the right areas, property can provide security and an income. I would advise any young person to either use their work to get on the property ladder or to look at buying some property that needs some refurbishment work, doing the work and adding some value. Once you've added value, sell it and move on to the next. Someone working their way up the corporate ladder can go on to become a millionaire through property if they want to and still have the safety and the security of a job.

Another piece of advice I give to younger people is to start a pension. Financial planning is important at any age, even when you are in your early twenties and indestructible! I started my pension at the age of twenty-five. A pension enables you to protect yourself in the future and reduces your tax. In addition to that, it's a way of putting money away that you can't spend. If someone starts a pension at eighteen or nineteen years old, they can affordably and feasibly build a £1-million pot by retirement.

These are some of the practical tips I like to share with the people I meet who want to be successful. And let's face it, who doesn't want to be a success?

Success happens in stages, incrementally. It means different things to different people. Often, it's about financial success and riches. For much of my life, that was the focus. I wanted to be rich, I wanted the best things money could buy. That's not the sole driver for me now. Yes, I still strive to maintain a high level of wealth, but I also want to help people.

The representation of success and wealth can sometimes be negative in culture. Take Scrooge for example. He's the guy with all the money but none of the charm. He doesn't care about people. This is a common cultural trope.

But from my experience this stereotype is wrong. I've always found that the more successful people are, the more they tend to care about others. They have more, so they can give more. Typically, I find successful people like to give back and like helping other people.

Ultimately, we crave success because we hope that success will make us happy. And undoubtedly success can lead to happiness. It can lead to more money, better health, better relationships. But success per se doesn't equal happiness. I know plenty of people who would be classified as successful but who are unhappy.

I believe that personal growth is a bigger indicator of happiness than success. In life, you're either growing or you're dying. I know that I feel happier when I'm growing, when I'm learning, when I feel like I'm making the most out of my life.

Personal growth is about feeding your mind, opening yourself up to new ideas and experiences and improving yourself. Success allows me the practical things I need in order to grow. It allows me to have those experiences that make me happy: the holidays, the Michelin-starred meals, the designer clothes.

The secret to ultimate success, maybe then, is to follow the four stages and live a life in which you've tried, you've applied yourself, you've learned, grown, and done right by yourself and others and you've been the best version of yourself that you can be. That, to me, looks like a very successful endeavour indeed.